The Riverside Literature Series

# POEMS AND STORIES

BY

BRET HARTE

SELECTED AND EDITED FOR SCHOOLS AND COLLEGES
WITH AN INTRODUCTION

BY

CHARLES SWAIN THOMAS, A.M.
*Head of the English Department in the*
*Newton (Mass.) High School*

BOSTON NEW YORK CHICAGO
HOUGHTON MIFFLIN COMPANY
The Riverside Press Cambridge

# CONTENTS





The Riverside Press
CAMBRIDGE . MASSACHUSETTS

# PREFACE

WHILE Bret Harte has been famous for nearly half a century, comparatively few students of the present generation have any conception of the amount or the versatility of his writings. His collected works in the Riverside Edition comprise nineteen volumes, and embrace sketches, essays, short stories, novels, poems, and one drama. In order to give students of school and college some adequate idea of the extent and variety and method of this work, this volume of selections has been prepared. It is hoped that the Introduction and the Notes will suggest further reading and thus acquaint the student, not only with the author's art, but also with the incidents and characters of that romantic civilization of California which is rapidly passing away from the memory of the living.

For the biographical data of the Introduction the editor is largely indebted to Henry C. Merwin's *Life of Bret Harte.*

C. S. T.

Newton, Massachusetts,
June, 1912.

# INTRODUCTION

## BRET HARTE

## 1836–1902

If we were asked to account for the breadth of sympathy which Bret Harte displayed in his life and writing, we should undoubtedly be aided in our answer by the knowledge that his paternal grandfather was a Jew, his paternal grandmother a member of the Dutch Church, his father a Catholic, and his mother an Episcopalian. His wide experience in travel, both at home and abroad, his extensive acquaintance with men of various ranks — from the roughest miner of the Far West to the most courtly and the most cultivated men of America and of Europe — all this helped to deepen and to widen this cosmopolitan attitude. Deeply immersed as he was for years in the spirit that the Forty-Niners created, Bret Harte never allowed the provincialism of his surroundings to deaden the force of this liberal sympathy.

### Ancestry and Boyhood

Francis Brett Harte — such was his baptismal name — was born in Albany, New York, on August 25, 1836. When as a young man he entered upon his career as a journalist and short-story writer, he dropped the Francis, clipped the final *t* from Brett, and won renown under the shortened name of Bret Harte. And as such he will always be known.

Bret Harte's father's name was Henry Harte. The father was educated at Union College, Schenectady, and became an accomplished scholar, especially proficient as a linguist.

He married Elizabeth Rebecca Ostrander, a member of a prominent Dutch family. Mr. and Mrs. Harte seem to have led a roving and unsettled life. Mr. Harte was, at the time of the birth of Francis Brett, a teacher in Albany, where he remained three or four years. From Albany the family went to Hudson, New York, and later lived — generally for short periods — in turn at New Brunswick, New Jersey, at Philadelphia, at Providence, Lowell, Boston, and elsewhere. Mr. Harte died in 1845.

At the time of his father's death Francis was nine years old, — the youngest of four children — two daughters and two sons. They, with their mother, lived for several years in New York and Brooklyn, supported by relatives. Later all except the elder daughter moved to California.

Bret Harte attended various schools up to his thirteenth year and then his academic life ceased. The atmosphere of his father's home, where an unerring literary taste reigned, provided his richest experience. At a very early age he acquired a fondness for Shakespeare and Froissart, and developed his liking for the best by further reading in Cervantes, Fielding, Smollett, Goldsmith, Dickens, and Irving.

### On the Pacific Slope, 1854–1871

Soon after her arrival in California Mrs. Harte was married to Colonel Andrew Williams, a highly cultivated gentleman, who had been a college friend of her former husband. With his mother and stepfather Bret Harte, who was then eighteen, lived for over a year, occupying part of his time in teaching and part as clerk to an apothecary in San Francisco.

When Bret Harte left Colonel Williams's house in 1856 he was twenty years old. He first became tutor for a family at Alamo. Later he became an express messenger on stages which ran between Humboldt Bay and Del Norte, in the extreme northern portion of California — an experience which finds frequent reflection in his stories — particularly in the famous character of Yuba Bill, the California stage-driver. After this engagement as expressman, Bret Harte became a printer at Union, California, in the office of the *Humboldt Times.* He also did some teaching, and for a short period was again clerk for an apothecary. Just before his return to San Francisco in 1856 he was assistant editor of the *Northern California*, a paper published at Eureka.

His editorial career at Eureka had an abrupt close. The editor had gone away and had left Bret Harte in charge. During the unfortunate absence certain white men near Eureka had inflicted a cowardly massacre upon a group of Indians. The temporary editor scathingly condemned the outrage, and the editorial in turn violently aroused the wrath of the American community. A mob, quickly formed, was intent on destroying the office and wreaking vengeance on the writer. Bret Harte armed himself to meet the issue, and on the night of the expected attack, sat at his desk with loaded pistols within easy reach. The fortunate arrival of government cavalry averted the threatened danger. The regular editor on his return to Eureka made peace with his *clientèle* by immediately dismissing from his employ the writer of the offensive article, and thus left Bret Harte free to return to the safer refuge of San Francisco.

This was in 1857. The fourteen succeeding years, which ended with his departure to the East, made Bret Harte the most distinguished literary man in California. His writings during these years of distinctive authorship, while they analyzed in trenchant severity the rawness of that mining period, nevertheless spread over the entire state a glamour which charmingly revealed the primitive and elemental manhood of those mining pioneers. Let us record some of the successive tasks which he performed and some of the successful triumphs which his endeavor won.

When Bret Harte returned to San Francisco in 1857 he secured employment as typesetter in the office of a newspaper — the *Golden Era*, edited by an amiable gentleman named Laurence. But the young man's interest was not long confined to mere typesetting. He yearned to see his own productions in print. This pleasure he had had when as a lad of eleven he had secretly mailed a poem — *Autumnal Musings* — to the *New York Sunday Atlas;* and he had rejoiced when he saw this poem published in the succeeding issue of that paper. His work on the *Northern California*, though ending in local ignominy, had nevertheless sharpened his talents and aroused his ambition. Accordingly when he found that the moments transferred from mechanical to creative composition met with editorial encouragement, he grew more industrious and more efficient. He was so successful that he was soon given a desk in the editorial room, and thus he began in earnest his career as an author. The *Golden Era*, fortunately, was not merely a purveyor of news — its instincts were literary as well. In its pages were published many of those sketches later preserved in Bret Harte's collected works — *In a Balcony*, *A Boy's Dog*, *Sidewalkings*, and the earlier *Condensed Novels.*

Feeling now assured of a reliable income, Bret Harte married in 1862 Miss Anna Griswold, whose parents lived in New York City. To this union four children were born, two sons, Griswold and Francis King, and two daughters, Jessemy and Ethel.

Two years after his marriage, Bret Harte was appointed secretary of the California Mint. This position he held for six years, and as his duties were not arduous he was able all the while to continue his literary work. In 1867 he published a volume of poems, the *Condensed Novels*, and his *Bohemian Papers.*

In 1868 Anton Roman, a San Francisco bookseller, founded the *Overland Monthly* and asked Bret Harte to become the editor. To the initial number Bret Harte contributed two poems, — *San Francisco* and *The Return of Belisarius.* The second number was the more significant, for it contained *The Luck of Roaring Camp*, which won the attention of James T. Fields, who invited Mr. Harte to write for the *Atlantic Monthly* a story in the same vein.

Perhaps the production which contributed most to Bret Harte's fame was *Plain Language from Truthful James*, more commonly entitled *The Heathen Chinee.* This poem immediately caught the popular ear and was universally quoted. The author's attitude toward this effort is proof of his critical discernment, for he set little store by it.

Indeed he at first refused it a place in the *Overland*, and finally published it only when strongly urged by Ambrose Bierce and other friends whose literary judgment he valued. The poem still has currency, due far more to its acquired momentum than to its inherent literary value, though its satire and its cleverness are obvious.

Among Bret Harte's many friends of this period were Thomas Starr King, whose devotion to the North helped to save California to the Union; Mrs. Jessie Benton Frémont, wife of John C. Frémont; Charles N. Stoddard, the author, and Mark Twain, who was then a reporter on the *Morning Call* and who was just coming into public notice.

Bret Harte has written his early impression of Mark Twain's powers as a story-teller as revealed in one of the latter's earlier visits: —

"In the course of the conversation he remarked that the unearthly laziness that prevailed in the town he had been visiting was beyond anything in his previous experience. He said the men did nothing all day long but sit around the barroom stove, spit, and 'swop lies.' He spoke in a low satiric drawl, which was in itself irresistible. He went on to tell one of those extravagant stories, and half unconsciously dropped into the lazy tone and manner of the original narrator. I asked him to tell it again to a friend who came in, and then asked him to write it out for the *Californian.* He did so, and when published it was an emphatic success. It was the first work of his that had attracted general attention, and it crossed the Sierras for an Eastern reading. The story was *The Jumping Frog of Caleveras.* It is now known and laughed over, I suppose, wherever the English language is spoken, but it will never be as funny to any one in print as it was to me, told for the first time by the unknown Twain himself on that morning in the San Francisco Mint."

There are many other incidents in Bret Harte's California experience on which the biographer would willingly pause, for he does not weary of them as Bret Harte himself wearied of them.

Such weariness on Bret Harte's part was obviously not

due to any lack of prosperity or of friendly appreciation; for his fame was firmly established. He was recognized everywhere as the skillful literary exponent of California life; he still maintained his profitable secretaryship at the Mint; he was a member of the English faculty at the University of California, the Editor of the successful *Overland*, and the centre of a most congenial coterie. But voices urgent and alluring were calling him, and in February, 1871, he took final leave of a city and a society whose varied phases he had so vividly portrayed. The eight intimate friends — all fellow craftsmen — who gave him his farewell dinner later had keenly to regret the complete severance of these ties, for Mr. Harte was averse to letter-writing and in the future months and years there was almost no communication between them. In leaving California, however, Bret Harte took with him the memory of the gigantic coarseness and the elemental virtues of that pioneer life which was to be the inspiration for many a future sketch and story.

### On the Atlantic Coast — 1871-1878

Bret Harte's objective destination was New York, though he stopped at Chicago where a group of men had hoped to induce him to accept the editorship of the *Lakeside Monthly*. Bret Harte evidently was not much interested in the project, for he carelessly broke his promise to meet the promoters at the dinner which had been arranged for him. He hurried on to New York to the home of his sister, Mrs. F. F. Knaufft, where, during the next two years, he and his family remained, except for occasional visits elsewhere.

Soon after his arrival in New York he went with his wife and children to Boston, or rather to Cambridge, to be the guests for a week at the home of W. D. Howells, at that time assistant editor of the *Atlantic Monthly*. In Cambridge and in Boston Bret Harte was most cordially received. He met Lowell, Emerson, Longfellow, and many other literary men of that group. He seems to have been a bit disappointed in Boston; the transfer from the crude and unconventional life of the California redwood forest and San Francisco Bohemianism to the refinements of Harvard

College and of Beacon Hill was perhaps too sudden to prevent a certain vague confusion of culture and hypocrisy. The visit, however, was a financial success; it was at least partially responsible for the contract he later made with James R. Osgood and Company, then publishers of the *Atlantic Monthly*, by which they agreed to pay Bret Harte $10,000 for whatever stories or poems he would write for them during the ensuing year. The stories written and published under this agreement were: *The Poet of Sierra Flat*, *Princess Bob and her Friends*, *The Romance of the Madroño Hollow*, and *How Santa Claus Came to Simpson's Bar*. Besides these were the poems: *A Greyport Legend*, *A Newport Romance*, *Concepcion de Arguello*, *Grandmother Tenterden*, and *The Idyl of Battle Hollow*.

The next seven years of Bret Harte's life—from February, 1871, when he arrived in New York, to June, 1878, when he departed for Crefeld, Prussia, where he was to be United States Commercial Agent — were spent largely in New York. He lived at various times in Newport; Morristown, New Jersey; New London, Connecticut; Cohasset, Massachusetts, and Sea Cliff, Long Island. A portion of his time he spent in lecturing, journeying as far west as St. Louis. He was chiefly occupied, however, in writing novels, short stories, sketches, poems, and plays.

Notwithstanding the high prices he received for much of this material, he was temperamentally unfit to manage his funds judiciously; continued financial troubles, therefore, came to him and his family. Always harassed by debt and habitually restive under the lack of ready money, he was glad to accept from President Hayes the Crefeld appointment, which his influential friends secured for him. Leaving his family at Sea Cliff, he sailed in June, 1878, and never returned to America. So far as the world knows it was also the final parting with his wife, though the cause of the separation has, fortunately, never been disclosed.

### Consular Service — 1878-1885

When Bret Harte first landed in Crefeld, he keenly felt the loneliness of his situation. However, he was somewhat cheered one day as he was passing a bookstore to catch sight of a volume bearing the familiar name of *Bret Harte.* Examination showed it to be a German translation of selected stories, and the sight of this helped to dissipate his feeling of isolation.

Bret Harte's official duties as Consul seem to have been performed with reasonable satisfaction, but he never acquired any genuine affection for the place or for the work. He was lonely; his health was not robust; he was hampered by a limited knowledge of the German language; and he finally sought relief from the tedium in a rather extended vacation in England.

His main purpose in going to England was to meet James Anthony Froude, the noted historian and essayist. The two became fast friends, and Harte remained for some time a guest in Froude's home. While in England he brought out a volume of stories and poems, and also delivered several successful lectures.

Mr. Merwin, in his life of Bret Harte, names the following as the product of the author's two-years' residence in Crefeld: *A Legend of Sammstadt, The Indiscretion of Elsbeth, Views from a German Spion,* and *Unser Karl.*

In 1880, Bret Harte, at his request for a transfer, was appointed to the consulship at Glasgow, where the salary was larger, and where life was more congenial to the author's taste. He was, however, frequently drawn down to London, for which city he had acquired a strong predilection. Notwithstanding these frequent visits he seems to have satisfied the Government at Washington that he was doing his work satisfactorily, though rumors reached the Department that he was too often absent from his post.

His work as an author went steadily onward, and he was likewise able to make some literary friendships. His most noted friends were the two novelists, William Black and Walter Besant.

Bret Harte held the consulship at Glasgow until 1885. The defeat of the Republican party and the election of Grover Cleveland forced his retirement.

### Residence in London — 1885-1902

Bret Harte has been criticized for not returning to America. Doubtless he might have done so after being relieved of his consular post in Glasgow. There may have been family reasons; his second son had married in England and settled in a home where the father was a frequent visitor; perhaps he felt that his literary work in England might be more remunerative; it may be that he was strongly held by the glamor of London and the friendships of Londoners. Whatever the reason, we may know that it was not because of any lack of patriotic devotion to the land of his birth, for he was always a strong defender of America and of American ideals. But to the day of his death he persistently kept his residence in England, not even returning to visit his relatives or those friends of his who had rejoiced at his earlier successes. He seems to have been temperamentally averse to going back and picking up the dropped threads of the past.

During the first ten years of his life in London — from 1885 to 1895 — he made his home with M. Arthur and Mme. Van de Velde, friends who had been first attracted to him by the admiration they had for his literary work. He remained with them until the death of M. Van de Velde, and then engaged rooms at 74 Lancaster Gate. Here he kept his lodgings until his death in 1902.

He had many friends in England who freely extended to him their hospitality. He sought mild forms of diversion, part of the time in traveling on the Continent; but he found his highest joy in his work — interested in the companionship of the new characters he was all the time creating, but more fascinated by the company of such old associates as Jack Hamlin and Colonel Starbottle. He grew to love his art, and to it he was glad to devote his patiently unremitting endeavor.

During the last months of his life Bret Harte was troubled greatly by cancer of the throat. A surgical operation gave only temporary relief. He kept valiantly at his work. One day in April, 1902, he seated himself at his desk and wrote the beginning of a new tale of Colonel Starbottle, but this he was never to finish. He lingered until May 5, when he was suddenly attacked with a severe hemorrhage of the throat and died a few hours later. The only persons at his bedside were his physicians, Mme. Van de Velde, and her servants. His wife and children were in attendance at his funeral a few days later.

### Critical Estimate

The Puritan temperament is not likely to grant full justice to Bret Harte's work, for Bret Harte admits to his pages themes which a punctilious nature would reject. In depicting the wild and brutally immoral life of the western mining-camp he painted things as they were; and his realism — tinctured always with idealism — required the vivid portrayal of the criminal act and the liberal use of the unchastened epithet. Such acts loom so large and such epithets roar so loud that the over-scrupulous retreat in quick alarm.

Should these critics read more deeply they would discover that the author had conceived his task to be that of the truthful teller of a truthful tale, and that his word must therefore be cousin to the deed. He himself is an unimpassioned witness; he stands aloof — not uninterested, not unsympathetic — but certainly not a canting moralist who is portraying the redness of vice in order to warn evildoers from the mouth of hell-gate. If virtue triumphs, it triumphs not because it may point a moral, but because it may adorn a tale. You may not like the ethics, but you should admit the art.

Furthermore, you will usually find on close examination that the ethics is sound. The charm of the story is often, as in *The Luck of Roaring Camp*, the diffusing essence of a barbaric tenderness, which a grim and profane exterior cannot encase. It comes out surely, though unostentatiously. Or it may be, as in *Tennessee's Partner*, an abiding sense of loyalty — friend to friend — that is all the more engaging because it is so manifestly unpretentious, — performed as a matter of course without thought of virtuous doing and apparently without struggle. Indeed one of the marked traits in most of the characters that Bret Harte has made famous, is what I may call their intuitive act. Colonel Starbottle, Jack Hamlin, Mr. Oakhurst, Dr. Duchesne — each performs unquestioningly in all his varied situations the deed which a certain grim fatality seems to exact with an unanalyzed but predetermined nicety. Their thoughts and acts are weirdly direct. They may be moral, immoral or unmoral; but their reaction is immediate.

Of other characters, however, this is not always so. In one of the very best of the later stories — *Left Out on Lone Star Mountain* — we see John Ford, the attractive young prospector, in a moment of wavering, tempted to appropriate to himself a mass of virgin gold which is legally his, but which rightfully belongs jointly to him and his four partners. The moral victory is gained, and John Ford hurries away to call back his deserting partners to share the newfound vein which a sudden slide had disclosed. The moral victory is no less great because of the fact that on their return they find that a second slide has carried the treasure completely away and again left them destitute.

Chesterton and other critics have pointed out that Bret Harte's humor is of the minimizing sort, whereas American humor is of the exaggerating sort. Bret Harte tells in *The Society upon the Stanislaus* of the row that interrupted an evening's program of their literary society and killed, or at least rendered unconscious, one Abner Dean: —

Then Abner Dean of Angel's raised a point of order, when
A chunk of old red sandstone took him in the abdomen,
And he smiled a kind of sickly smile, and curled up on the floor,
And the subsequent proceedings interested him no more.

This last line is of course an absurd understatement, but it is so markedly understated that the real truth is as obviously wrenched as if it were greatly exaggerated. Really the humors are not of two types; they are variants of the same type. Bret Harte generally prefers the quiet smile that such minimizing provokes.

A prevailing element of charm in humor is its unexpectedness — an unlooked-for turn. Colonel Starbottle is very much disgusted at the way a certain dispute is carried on between two miners. He characterized it as "a fuss that gentlemen might have settled in ten minutes over a social glass, ef they meant business; or in ten seconds with a revolver, ef they meant fun."

These same miners — York and Scott — kept up a long dispute. They became rival candidates for the California Legislature, and the two former friends and partners engaged in a bitter mud-slinging campaign. York delivered his first philippic to a crowd in which Scott was an interested listener. Scott's past was mercilessly exposed. When York finished, Scott was pushed to the platform: —

> As his frowsy head and unkempt beard appeared above the railing, it was evident that he was drunk. But it was also evident, before he opened his lips, that the orator of Sandy Bar . . . stood before them. A consciousness of this power lent a certain dignity to his figure. . . . "There 's naught, gentlemen," said Scott, leaning forward on the railing, — "there 's naught as that man hez said as is n't true. I *was* run outer Cairo; I *did* belong to the Regulators; I *did* desert from the army; I *did* leave a wife in Kansas. But there 's one thing he did n't charge me with, and maybe he 's forgotten. For three years, gentlemen, I was that man's partner."

This element of humor, occurring again and again in the speeches of Yuba Bill, Jack Hamlin, Colonel Starbottle, Truthful James, and others has been generally recognized as an element in Bret Harte distinctly characteristic, but the beauty of Bret Harte's language has received scant notice. Perhaps this may be explained by the fact that he has had few critics, and that his readers have for the most part been hasty in their pursuit of story; they have read principally for the pleasure of plot and situation and not for the pleasure of style. Yet to one who reads leisurely, the perception of this sense of language-beauty is as gratifying as it is obvious. Who of our great masters of prose style could have written a better description than the one which narrates the passage of that crude funeral cart which carried the body of Tennessee's partner from the gallows to the grave?[1]

[1] See page 60.

More softly melodious though not so trenchantly vivid is that paragraph in *The Outcasts of Poker Flat* which describes the death-surroundings of innocent Piney Woods and the sin-stained Duchess.[1]

Marked as is the melody of his prose, the quality is even more obvious in his verse. His sense of rhythm is so perfect that it does not desert him even when he allows the rough miners of the camp to voice their thoughts dramatically in the crude dialect of the Forty-Niners. In addition to the faultless rhythm, there is a skilled assembling of vocalic and consonantal effects that gives a satisfying sense of melody and harmony. This is beautifully wrought out in one of the lyrics of *Cadet Grey.*

NOT YET

*Not yet, O friend, not yet! the patient stars*
*Lean from their lattices, content to wait.*
*All is illusion till the morning bars*
*Slip from the levels of the Eastern gate.*
*Night is too young, O friend! day is too near;*
*Wait for the day that maketh all things clear.*
*Not yet, O friend, not yet!*

*Not yet, O love, not yet! all is not true,*
*All is not ever as it seemeth now.*
*Soon shall the river take another blue,*
*Soon dies yon light upon the mountain brow.*
*What lieth dark, O love, bright day will fill.*
*Wait for thy morning, be it good or ill.*
*Not yet, O love, not yet!*

Some critics have commented upon Bret Harte's paganism, his aloofness from the sense of mystery, and his spiritual indifference. This censure is not quite deserved, and any reader of such of his poems as *Relieving Guard* or *The Angelus* will see why it is not deserved. He does not, to be sure, dwell long on the mystery of human life. No one would call him a mystic, or a "subtle asserter of the soul," but he has written enough to prove that his soul

[1] See p. 50.

did, at times, throb in unison with the highest of high themes. That he chose other chords for his more constant music does, however, suggest a lack of abundant spiritual resource. His habitual realm of art was circumscribed.

This fact helps us to prophesy concerning the relative rank of his poetry and his short stories. Great poetry demands a more constant lingering upon spiritual themes and a more habitual voicing of the haunting of mystery and "high seriousness." Stories may or may not breathe the softer strains of such indwelling. Certainly they do not demand it. We may say, then, that Bret Harte lacks in the habit of thought the one great requisite for great poetry. On the other hand, he lacks none of the art-demands of the short story. The power of immediate entry, keen conception of character and situation, skill in staging the action, ability to move his characters toward and away, a faultless sense of humor and of pathos, a deft selection of the inevitable word — all these he has and has in abundant reserve. It is certain that as we study his writings we shall eventually come to respect the persisting talent revealed in his verse and to admire the flashes of genius revealed in his stories.

# POEMS

## JOHN BURNS OF GETTYSBURG

Have you heard the story that gossips tell
Of Burns of Gettysburg? — No? Ah, well:
Brief is the glory that hero earns,
Briefer the story of poor John Burns.
He was the fellow who won renown, —
The only man who did n't back down
When the rebels rode through his native town;
But held his own in the fight next day,
When all his townsfolk ran away.
That was in July sixty-three,
The very day that General Lee,
Flower of Southern chivalry,
Baffled and beaten, backward reeled
From a stubborn Meade and a barren field.

I might tell how but the day before
John Burns stood at his cottage door,
Looking down the village street,
Where, in the shade of his peaceful vine,
He heard the low of his gathered kine,
And felt their breath with incense sweet;
Or I might say, when the sunset burned
The old farm gable, he thought it turned
The milk that fell like a babbling flood
Into the milk-pail red as blood!
Or how he fancied the hum of bees
Were bullets buzzing among the trees.
But all such fanciful thoughts as these
Were strange to a practical man like Burns,

Who minded only his own concerns,
Troubled no more by fancies fine
Than one of his calm-eyed, long-tailed kine, —
Quite old-fashioned and matter-of-fact,
Slow to argue, but quick to act.
That was the reason, as some folk say,
He fought so well on that terrible day.

And it was terrible. On the right
Raged for hours the heady fight,
Thundered the battery's double bass, —
Difficult music for men to face;
While on the left — where now the graves
Undulate like the living waves
That all that day unceasing swept
Up to the pits the rebels kept —
'Round shot ploughed the upland glades,
Sown with bullets, reaped with blades;
Shattered fences here and there
Tossed their splinters in the air;
The very trees were stripped and bare;
The barns that once held yellow grain
Were heaped with harvests of the slain;
The cattle bellowed on the plain,
The turkeys screamed with might and main,
And brooding barn-fowl left their rest
With strange shells bursting in each nest.

Just where the tide of battle turns,
Erect and lonely stood old John Burns.
How do you think the man was dressed?
He wore an ancient long buff vest,
Yellow as saffron, — but his best;
And buttoned over his manly breast
Was a bright blue coat, with a rolling collar,
And large gilt buttons, — size of a dollar, —

With tails that the country-folk called "swaller."
He wore a broad-brimmed, bell-crowned hat,
White as the locks on which it sat.
Never had such a sight been seen
For forty years on the village green,
Since old John Burns was a country beau,
And went to the "quiltings" long ago.

Close at his elbows all that day,
Veterans of the Peninsula,
Sunburnt and bearded, charged away;
And striplings, downy of lip and chin, —
Clerks that the Home Guard mustered in, —
Glanced, as they passed, at the hat he wore,
Then at the rifle his right hand bore,
And hailed him, from out their youthful lore,
With scraps of a slangy *répertoire:*
"How are you, White Hat?" "Put her through!"
"Your head's level!" and "Bully for you!"
Called him "Daddy," — begged he'd disclose
The name of the tailor who made his clothes,
And what was the value he set on those;
While Burns, unmindful of jeer and scoff,
Stood there picking the rebels off, —
With his long brown rifle and bell-crown hat,
And the swallow-tails they were laughing at.

'T was but a moment, for that respect
Which clothes all courage their voices checked;
And something the wildest could understand
Spake in the old man's strong right hand,
And his corded throat, and the lurking frown
Of his eyebrows under his old bell-crown;
Until, as they gazed, there crept in awe
Through the ranks in whispers, and some men saw,
In the antique vestments and long white hair,

The Past of the Nation in battle there;
And some of the soldiers since declare
That the gleam of his old white hat afar,
Like the crested plume of the brave Navarre,
That day was their oriflamme of war.

So raged the battle. You know the rest:
How the rebels, beaten and backward pressed,
Broke at the final charge and ran.
At which John Burns — a practical man —
Shouldered his rifle, unbent his brows,
And then went back to his bees and cows.

That is the story of old John Burns;
This is the moral the reader learns:
In fighting the battle, the question 's whether
You 'll show a hat that 's white, or a feather!

## THE REVEILLE

Hark! I hear the tramp of thousands,
And of armèd men the hum;
Lo! a nation's hosts have gathered
Round the quick alarming drum, —
Saying, "Come,
Freemen, come!
Ere your heritage be wasted," said the quick alarming drum.

"Let me of my heart take counsel:
War is not of life the sum;
Who shall stay and reap the harvest
When the autumn days shall come?"
But the drum
Echoed, "Come!
Death shall reap the braver harvest," said the solemn-sounding drum.

"But when won the coming battle,
What of profit springs therefrom?
What if conquest, subjugation,
Even greater ills become?"
But the drum
Answered, "Come!
You must do the sum to prove it," said the Yankee answering drum.

"What if, 'mid the cannon's thunder,
Whistling shot and bursting bomb,
When my brothers fall around me,
Should my heart grow cold and numb?"
But the drum
Answered, "Come!
Better there in death united, than in life a recreant. — Come!"

Thus they answered, — hoping, fearing,
Some in faith, and doubting some,
Till a trumpet-voice proclaiming,
Said, "My chosen people, come!"
Then the drum,
Lo! was dumb,
For the great heart of the nation, throbbing, answered, "Lord, we come!"

## RELIEVING GUARD

THOMAS STARR KING. OBIIT MARCH 4, 1864

CAME the relief. "What, sentry, ho!
How passed the night through thy long waking?"
"Cold, cheerless, dark, — as may befit
The hour before the dawn is breaking."

"No sight? no sound?" "No; nothing save
The plover from the marshes calling,
And in yon western sky, about
An hour ago, a star was falling."

"A star? There 's nothing strange in that."
"No, nothing; but, above the thicket,
Somehow it seemed to me that God
Somewhere had just relieved a picket."

## ON A PEN OF THOMAS STARR KING

This is the reed the dead musician dropped,
With tuneful magic in its sheath still hidden;
The prompt allegro of its music stopped,
Its melodies unbidden.

But who shall finish the unfinished strain,
Or wake the instrument to awe and wonder,
And bid the slender barrel breathe again,
An organ-pipe of thunder!

His pen! what humbler memories cling about
Its golden curves! what shapes and laughing graces
Slipped from its point, when his full heart went out
In smiles and courtly phrases?

The truth, half jesting, half in earnest flung;
The word of cheer, with recognition in it;
The note of alms, whose golden speech outrung
The golden gift within it.

But all in vain the enchanter's wand we wave:
No stroke of ours recalls his magic vision:
The incantation that its power gave
Sleeps with the dead magician.

# ANNIVERSARY POEM

DELIVERED ON THE FOURTEENTH ANNIVERSARY OF CALIFORNIA'S ADMISSION INTO THE UNION, SEPTEMBER 9, 1864

We meet in peace, though from our native East
The sun that sparkles on our birthday feast
Glanced as he rose on fields whose dews were red
With darker tints than those Aurora spread.
Though shorn his rays, his welcome disk concealed
In the dim smoke that veiled each battlefield,
Still striving upward, in meridian pride,
He climbed the walls that East and West divide, —
Saw his bright face flashed back from golden sand,
And Sapphire seas that lave the Western land.

Strange was the contrast that such scenes disclose
From his high vantage o'er eternal snows;
There War's alarm the brazen trumpet rings —
Here his love-song the mailed cicala sings;
There bayonets glitter through the forest glades —
Here yellow cornfields stack their peaceful blades;
There the deep trench where Valor finds a grave —
Here the long ditch that curbs the peaceful wave;
There the bold sapper with his lighted train —
Here the dark tunnel and its stores of gain;
Here the full harvest and the wain's advance —
There the Grim Reaper and the ambulance.

With scenes so adverse, what mysterious bond
Links our fair fortunes to the shores beyond?
Why come we here — last of a scattered fold —
To pour new metal in the broken mould?
To yield our tribute, stamped with Cæsar's face,
To Cæsar. stricken in the market-place?

Ah! love of country is the secret tie
That joins these contrasts 'neath one arching sky;
Though brighter paths our peaceful steps explore,
We meet together at the Nation's door.
War winds her horn, and giant cliffs go down
Like the high walls that girt the sacred town,
And bares the pathway to her throbbing heart,
From clustered village and from crowded mart.

Part of God's providence it was to found
A Nation's bulwark on this chosen ground;
Not Jesuit's zeal nor pioneer's unrest
Planted these pickets in the distant West,
But He who first the Nation's fate forecast
Placed here His fountains sealed for ages past,
Rock-ribbed and guarded till the coming time
Should fit the people for their work sublime;
When a new Moses with his rod of steel
Smote the tall cliffs with one wide-ringing peal,
And the old miracle in record told
To the new Nation was revealed in gold.

Judge not too idly that our toils are mean,
Though no new levies marshal on our green;
Nor deem too rashly that our gains are small,
Weighed with the prizes for which heroes fall.
See, where thick vapor wreathes the battle-line;
There Mercy follows with her oil and wine;
Or where brown Labor with its peaceful charm
Stiffens the sinews of the Nation's arm.
What nerves its hands to strike a deadlier blow
And hurl its legions on the rebel foe?
Lo! for each town new rising o'er our State
See the foe's hamlet waste and desolate,
While each new factory lifts its chimney tall,
Like a fresh mortar trained on Richmond's wall.

For this, O brothers, swings the fruitful vine,
Spread our broad pastures with their countless kine:
For this o'erhead the arching vault springs clear,
Sunlit and cloudless for one half the year;
For this no snowflake, e'er so lightly pressed,
Chills the warm impulse of our mother's breast.
Quick to reply, from meadows brown and sere,
She thrills responsive to Spring's earliest tear;
Breaks into blossom, flings her loveliest rose
Ere the white crocus mounts Atlantic snows;
And the example of her liberal creed
Teaches the lesson that to-day we heed.

Thus ours the lot with peaceful, generous hand
To spread our bounty o'er the suffering land;
As the deep cleft in Mariposa's wall
Hurls a vast river splintering in its fall, —
Though the rapt soul who stands in awe below
Sees but the arching of the promised bow, —
Lo! the far streamlet drinks its dews unseen,
And the whole valley wakes a brighter green.

## A SANITARY MESSAGE

LAST night, above the whistling wind,
  I heard the welcome rain, —
A fusillade upon the roof,
  A tattoo on the pane:
The keyhole piped; the chimney-top
  A warlike trumpet blew;
Yet, mingling with these sounds of strife,
  A softer voice stole through.

"Give thanks, O brothers!" said the voice,
  "That He who sent the rains
Hath spared your fields the scarlet dew
  That drips from patriot veins:

I 've seen the grass on Eastern graves
In brighter verdure rise;
But, oh! the rain that gave it life
Sprang first from human eyes.

"I come to wash away no stain
Upon your wasted lea;
I raise no banners, save the ones
The forest waves to me:
Upon the mountain side, where Spring
Her farthest picket sets,
My reveille awakes a host
Of grassy bayonets.

"I visit every humble roof;
I mingle with the low;
Only upon the highest peaks
My blessings fall in snow;
Until, in tricklings of the stream
And drainings of the lea,
My unspent bounty comes at last
To mingle with the sea."

And thus all night, above the wind,
I heard the welcome rain, —
A fusillade upon the roof,
A tattoo on the pane:
The keyhole piped; the chimney-top
A warlike trumpet blew:
But, mingling with these sounds of strife,
This hymn of peace stole through.

# CHIQUITA

BEAUTIFUL! Sir, you may say so. Thar is n't her match in the county;
Is thar, old gal, — Chiquita, my darling, my beauty?
Feel of that neck, sir, — thar 's velvet! Whoa! steady, — ah, will you, you vixen!
Whoa! I say. Jack, trot her out; let the gentleman look at her paces.

Morgan! — she ain't nothing else, and I 've got the papers to prove it.
Sired by Chippewa Chief, and twelve hundred dollars won't buy her.
Briggs of Tuolumne owned her. Did you know Briggs of Tuolumne?
Busted hisself in White Pine, and blew out his brains down in 'Frisco?

Hed n't no savey, hed Briggs. Thar, Jack! that 'll do, — quit that foolin'!
Nothin' to what she kin do, when she 's got her work cut out before her.
Hosses is hosses, you know, and likewise, too, jockeys is jockeys:
And 't ain't ev'ry man as can ride as knows what a hoss has got in him.

Know the old ford on the Fork, that nearly got Flanigan's leaders?
Nasty in daylight, you bet, and a mighty rough ford in low water!
Well, it ain't six weeks ago that me and the Jedge and his nevey

Struck for that ford in the night, in the rain, and the water all round us:

Up to our flanks in the gulch, and Rattlesnake Creek just a-bilin',
Not a plank left in the dam, and nary a bridge on the river.
I had the gray, and the Jedge had his roan, and his nevey, Chiquita;
And after us trundled the rocks jest loosed from the top of the cañon.

Lickity, lickity, switch, we came to the ford, and Chiquita
Buckled right down to her work, and, afore I could yell to her rider,
Took water jest at the ford, and there was the Jedge and me standing,
And twelve hundred dollars of hoss-flesh afloat, and a-driftin' to thunder!

Would ye b'lieve it? That night, that hoss, that 'ar filly, Chiquita,
Walked herself into her stall, and stood there, all quiet and dripping:
Clean as a beaver or rat, with nary a buckle of harness,
Just as she swam the Fork, — that hoss, that 'ar filly, Chiquita.

That 's what I call a hoss! and — What did you say? — Oh, the nevey?
Drownded, I reckoned, — leastways, he never kem back to deny it.
Ye see the derned fool had no seat, ye could n't have made him a rider;
And then, ye know, boys will be boys, and hosses — well, hosses is hosses!

# PLAIN LANGUAGE FROM TRUTHFUL JAMES

(TABLE MOUNTAIN, 1870)

WHICH I wish to remark,
  And my language is plain,
That for ways that are dark
  And for tricks that are vain,
The heathen Chinee is peculiar,
  Which the same I would rise to explain.

Ah Sin was his name;
  And I shall not deny,
In regard to the same,
  What that name might imply;
But his smile it was pensive and childlike,
  As I frequent remarked to Bill Nye.

It was August the third,
  And quite soft was the skies;
Which it might be inferred
  That Ah Sin was likewise;
Yet he played it that day upon William
  And me in a way I despise.

Which we had a small game,
  And Ah Sin took a hand.
It was Euchre. The same
  He did not understand;
But he smiled as he sat by the table,
  With the smile that was childlike and bland.

Yet the cards they were stocked
  In a way that I grieve,
And my feelings were shocked

At the state of Nye's sleeve,
Which was stuffed full of aces and bowers,
And the same with intent to deceive.

But the hands that were played
By that heathen Chinee,
And the points that he made,
Were quite frightful to see, —
Till at last he put down a right bower,
Which the same Nye had dealt unto me.

Then I looked up at Nye,
And he gazed upon me;
And he rose with a sigh,
And said, "Can this be?
We are ruined by Chinese cheap labor," —
And he went for that heathen Chinee.

In the scene that ensued
I did not take a hand,
But the floor it was strewed
Like the leaves on the strand
With the cards that Ah Sin had been hiding,
In the game "he did not understand."

In his sleeves, which were long,
He had twenty-four packs, —
Which was coming it strong,
Yet I state but the facts;
And we found on his nails, which were taper,
What is frequent in tapers, — that's wax.

Which is why I remark,
And my language is plain,
That for ways that are dark
And for tricks that are vain,
The heathen Chinee is peculiar, —
Which the same I am free to maintain.

## THE SOCIETY UPON THE STANISLAUS

I RESIDE at Table Mountain, and my name is Truthful James;
I am not up to small deceit or any sinful games;
And I'll tell in simple language what I know about the row
That broke up our Society upon the Stanislow.

But first I would remark, that it is not a proper plan
For any scientific gent to whale his fellow-man,
And, if a member don't agree with his peculiar whim,
To lay for that same member for to "put a head" on him.

Now nothing could be finer or more beautiful to see
Than the first six months' proceedings of that same Society,
Till Brown of Calaveras brought a lot of fossil bones
That he found within a tunnel near the tenement of Jones.

Then Brown he read a paper, and he reconstructed there,
From those same bones, an animal that was extremely rare;
And Jones then asked the Chair for a suspension of the rules,
Till he could prove that those same bones was one of his lost mules.

Then Brown he smiled a bitter smile, and said he was at fault,
It seemed he had been trespassing on Jones's family vault;
He was a most sarcastic man, this quiet Mr. Brown,
And on several occasions he had cleaned out the town.

Now I hold it is not decent for a scientific gent
To say another is an ass, — at least, to all intent;
Nor should the individual who happens to be meant
Reply by heaving rocks at him, to any great extent.

Then Abner Dean of Angel's raised a point of order, when
A chunk of old red sandstone took him in the abdomen,
And he smiled a kind of sickly smile, and curled up on the floor,
And the subsequent proceedings interested him no more.

For, in less time than I write it, every member did engage
In a warfare with the remnants of a palæozoic age;
And the way they heaved those fossils in their anger was a sin,
Till the skull of an old mammoth caved the head of Thompson in.

And this is all I have to say of these improper games,
For I live at Table Mountain, and my name is Truthful James;
And I 've told in simple language what I know about the row
That broke up our Society upon the Stanislow.

## A GREYPORT LEGEND

### (1797)

THEY ran through the streets of the seaport town,
They peered from the decks of the ships that lay;
The cold sea-fog that came whitening down
Was never as cold or white as they.
"Ho, Starbuck and Pinckney and Tenterden!
Run for your shallops, gather your men,
Scatter your boats on the lower bay."

Good cause for fear! In the thick mid-day
The hulk that lay by the rotting pier,
Filled with the children in happy play,
Parted its moorings and drifted clear,
Drifted clear beyond reach or call, —
Thirteen children they were in all, —
All adrift in the lower bay!

Said a hard-faced skipper, "God help us all!
She will not float till the turning tide!"
Said his wife, "My darling will hear *my* call,
Whether in sea or heaven she bide";
    And she lifted a quavering voice and high,
    Wild and strange as a sea-bird's cry,
        Till they shuddered and wondered at her side.

The fog drove down on each laboring crew,
Veiled each from each and the sky and shore:
There was not a sound but the breath they drew,
And the lap of water and creak of oar;
    And they felt the breath of the downs, fresh blown
    O'er leagues of clover and cold gray stone,
        But not from the lips that had gone before.

They came no more. But they tell the tale
That, when fogs are thick on the harbor reef,
The mackerel fishers shorten sail —
For the signal they know will bring relief;
    For the voices of children, still at play
    In a phantom hulk that drifts alway
        Through channels whose waters never fail.

It is but a foolish shipman's tale,
A theme for a poet's idle page;
But still, when the mists of Doubt prevail,
And we lie becalmed by the shores of Age,
    We hear from the misty troubled shore
    The voice of the children gone before,
        Drawing the soul to its anchorage.

## SAN FRANCISCO

### (FROM THE SEA)

SERENE, indifferent of Fate,
Thou sittest at the Western Gate;

Upon thy height, so lately won,
Still slant the banners of the sun;

Thou seest the white seas strike their tents,
O Warder of two continents!

And, scornful of the peace that flies
Thy angry winds and sullen skies,

Thou drawest all things, small or great,
To thee, beside the Western Gate.

. . . . . . . .

O lion's whelp, that hidest fast
In jungle growth of spire and mast!

I know thy cunning and thy greed,
Thy hard high lust and willful deed,

And all thy glory loves to tell
Of specious gifts material.

Drop down, O Fleecy Fog, and hide
Her skeptic sneer and all her pride!

Wrap her, O Fog, in gown and hood
Of her Franciscan Brotherhood.

Hide me her faults, her sin and blame;
With thy gray mantle cloak her shame!

So shall she, cowlèd, sit and pray
Till morning bears her sins away.

Then rise, O Fleecy Fog, and raise
The glory of her coming days;

Be as the cloud that flecks the seas
Above her smoky argosies;

When forms familiar shall give place
To stranger speech and newer face;

When all her throes and anxious fears
Lie hushed in the repose of years;

When Art shall raise and Culture lift
The sensual joys and meaner thrift,

And all fulfilled the vision we
Who watch and wait shall never see;

Who, in the morning of her race,
Toiled fair or meanly in our place,

But, yielding to the common lot,
Lie unrecorded and forgot.

## THE MOUNTAIN HEART'S-EASE

By scattered rocks and turbid waters shifting,
By furrowed glade and dell,
To feverish men thy calm, sweet face uplifting,
Thou stayest them to tell

The delicate thought that cannot find expression,
For ruder speech too fair,
That, like thy petals, trembles in possession,
And scatters on the air.

The miner pauses in his rugged labor,
And, leaning on his spade,
Laughingly calls unto his comrade-neighbor
To see thy charms displayed.

But in his eyes a mist unwonted rises,
And for a moment clear
Some sweet home face his foolish thought surprises,
And passes in a tear, —

Some boyish vision of his Eastern village,
Of uneventful toil,
Where golden harvests followed quiet tillage
Above a peaceful soil.

One moment only; for the pick, uplifting,
Through root and fibre cleaves,
And on the muddy current slowly drifting
Are swept by bruisèd leaves.

And yet, O poet in thy homely fashion,
Thy work thou dost fulfill,
For on the turbid current of his passion
Thy face is shining still.

## TO A SEA-BIRD

(SANTA CRUZ, 1869)

SAUNTERING hither on listless wings,
Careless vagabond of the sea,
Little thou heedest the surf that sings,
The bar that thunders, the shale that rings, —
Give me to keep thy company.

Little thou hast, old friend, that 's new;
Storms and wrecks are old things to thee;
Sick am I of these changes, too;
Little to care for, little to rue, —
I on the shore, and thou on the sea.

All of thy wanderings, far and near,
Bring thee at last to shore and me;
All of my journeyings end them here:
This our tether must be our cheer, —
I on the shore, and thou on the sea.

Lazily rocking on ocean's breast,
Something in common, old friend, have we:
Thou on the shingle seek'st thy nest,
I to the waters look for rest, —
I on the shore, and thou on the sea.

## WHAT THE CHIMNEY SANG

OVER the chimney the night-wind sang
And chanted a melody no one knew;
And the Woman stopped, as her babe she tossed,
And thought of the one she had long since lost,
And said, as her teardrops back she forced,
"I hate the wind in the chimney."

Over the chimney the night-wind sang
And chanted a melody no one knew;
And the Children said, as they closer drew,
"'T is some witch that is cleaving the black night through,
'T is a fairy trumpet that just then blew,
And we fear the wind in the chimney."

Over the chimney the night-wind sang
And chanted a melody no one knew;
And the Man, as he sat on his hearth below,
Said to himself, "It will surely snow,
And fuel is dear and wages low,
And I'll stop the leak in the chimney."

Over the chimney the night-wind sang
And chanted a melody no one knew;
But the Poet listened and smiled, for he
Was Man and Woman and Child, all three,
And said, "It is God's own harmony,
This wind we hear in the chimney."

## DICKENS IN CAMP

Above the pines the moon was slowly drifting,
The river sang below;
The dim Sierras, far beyond, uplifting
Their minarets of snow.

The roaring camp-fire, with rude humor, painted
The ruddy tints of health
On haggard face and form that drooped and fainted
In the fierce race for wealth;

Till one arose, and from his pack's scant treasure
A hoarded volume drew,
And cards were dropped from hands of listless leisure
To hear the tale anew.

And then, while round them shadows gathered faster,
And as the firelight fell,
He read aloud the book wherein the Master
Had writ of "Little Nell."

Perhaps 't was boyish fancy, — for the reader
Was youngest of them all, —
But, as he read, from clustering pine and cedar
A silence seemed to fall;

The fir-trees, gathering closer in the shadows,
Listened in every spray,
While the whole camp with "Nell" on English meadows
Wandered and lost their way.

And so in mountain solitudes — o'ertaken
As by some spell divine —
Their cares dropped from them like the needles shaken
From out the gusty pine.

Lost is that camp and wasted all its fire;
And he who wrought that spell?
Ah! towering pine and stately Kentish spire,
Ye have one tale to tell!

Lost is that camp, but let its fragrant story
Blend with the breath that thrills
With hop-vine's incense all the pensive glory
That fills the Kentish hills.

And on that grave where English oak and holly
And laurel wreaths entwine,
Deem it not all a too presumptuous folly,
This spray of Western pine!

*July*, 1870.

## THE MISSION BELLS OF MONTEREY

O BELLS that rang, O bells that sang
Above the martyrs' wilderness,
Till from that reddened coast-line sprang
The Gospel seed to cheer and bless,

What are your garnered sheaves to-day?
O Mission bells! Eleison bells!
O Mission bells of Monterey!

O bells that crash, O bells that clash
Above the chimney-crowded plain,
On wall and tower your voices dash,
But never with the old refrain;
In mart and temple gone astray!
Ye dangle bells! Ye jangle bells!
Ye wrangle bells of Monterey!

O bells that die, so far, so nigh,
Come back once more across the sea;
Not with the zealot's furious cry,
Not with the creed's austerity;
Come with His love alone to stay,
O Mission bells! Eleison bells!
O Mission bells of Monterey!

## THE ANGELUS

(HEARD AT THE MISSION DOLORES, 1868)

Bells of the Past, whose long-forgotten music
Still fills the wide expanse,
Tingeing the sober twilight of the Present
With color of romance!

I hear your call, and see the sun descending
On rock and wave and sand,
As down the coast the Mission voices, blending,
Girdle the heathen land.

Within the circle of your incantation
No blight nor mildew falls;
Nor fierce unrest, nor lust, nor low ambition
Passes those airy walls.

Borne on the swell of your long waves receding,
I touch the farther Past;
I see the dying glow of Spanish glory,
The sunset dream and last!

Before me rise the dome-shaped Mission towers,
The white Presidio;
The swart commander in his leathern jerkin,
The priest in stole of snow.

Once more I see Portolá's cross uplifting
Above the setting sun;
And past the headland, northward, slowly drifting,
The freighted galleon.

O solemn bells! whose consecrated masses
Recall the faith of old;
O tinkling bells! that lulled with twilight music!
The spiritual fold!

Your voices break and falter in the darkness, —
Break, falter, and are still;
And veiled and mystic, like the Host descending,
The sun sinks from the hill!

# STORIES AND SKETCHES

## THE LUCK OF ROARING CAMP

There was commotion in Roaring Camp. It could not have been a fight, for in 1850 that was not novel enough to have called together the entire settlement. The ditches and claims were not only deserted, but "Tuttle's grocery" had contributed its gamblers, who, it will be remembered, calmly continued their game the day that French Pete and Kanaka Joe shot each other to death over the bar in the front room. The whole camp was collected before a rude cabin on the outer edge of the clearing. Conversation was carried on in a low tone, but the name of a woman was frequently repeated. It was a name familiar enough in the camp, — "Cherokee Sal."

Perhaps the less said of her the better. She was a coarse and, it is to be feared, a very sinful woman. But at that time she was the only woman in Roaring Camp, and was just then lying in sore extremity, when she most needed the ministration of her own sex. Dissolute, abandoned, and irreclaimable, she was yet suffering a martyrdom hard enough to bear even when veiled by sympathizing womanhood, but now terrible in her loneliness. The primal curse had come to her in that original isolation which must have made the punishment of the first transgression so dreadful. It was, perhaps, part of the expiation of her sin that, at a moment when she most lacked her sex's intuitive tenderness and care, she met only the half-contemptuous faces of her masculine associates. Yet a few of the spectators were, I think, touched by her sufferings. Sandy Tipton thought it was "rough on Sal," and, in the contemplation of her condition, for a moment rose superior to the fact that he had an ace and two bowers in his sleeve.

It will be seen also that the situation was novel. Deaths were by no means uncommon in Roaring Camp, but a birth was a new thing. People had been dismissed the camp effectively, finally, and with no possibility of return; but this was the first time that anybody had been introduced *ab initio*. Hence the excitement.

"You go in there, Stumpy," said a prominent citizen known as "Kentuck," addressing one of the loungers. "Go in there, and see what you kin do. You've had experience in them things."

Perhaps there was a fitness in the selection. Stumpy, in other climes, had been the putative head of two families; in fact, it was owing to some legal informality in these proceedings that Roaring Camp — a city of refuge — was indebted to his company. The crowd approved the choice, and Stumpy was wise enough to bow to the majority. The door closed on the extempore surgeon and midwife, and Roaring Camp sat down outside, smoked its pipe, and awaited the issue.

The assemblage numbered about a hundred men. One or two of these were actual fugitives from justice, some were criminal, and all were reckless. Physically they exhibited no indication of their past lives and character. The greatest scamp had a Raphael face, with a profusion of blonde hair; Oakhurst, a gambler, had the melancholy air and intellectual abstraction of a Hamlet; the coolest and most courageous man was scarcely over five feet in height, with a soft voice and an embarrassed, timid manner. The term "roughs" applied to them was a distinction rather than a definition. Perhaps in the minor details of fingers, toes, ears, etc., the camp may have been deficient, but these slight omissions did not detract from their aggregate force. The strongest man had but three fingers on his right hand; the best shot had but one eye.

Such was the physical aspect of the men that were dispersed around the cabin. The camp lay in a triangular valley between two hills and a river. The only outlet was a steep trail over the summit of a hill that faced the cabin, now illuminated by the rising moon. The suffering woman might have seen it from the rude bunk whereon she lay, — seen it winding like a silver thread until it was lost in the stars above.

A fire of withered pine boughs added sociability to the gathering. By degrees the natural levity of Roaring Camp returned. Bets were freely offered and taken regarding the result. Three to five that "Sal would get through with it;" even that the child would survive; side bets as to the sex and complexion of the coming stranger. In the midst of an excited discussion an exclamation came from those nearest the door, and the camp stopped to listen. Above the swaying and moaning of the pines, the swift rush of the river, and the crackling of the fire rose a sharp, querulous cry, — a cry unlike anything heard before in the camp. The pines stopped moaning, the river ceased to rush, and the fire to crackle. It seemed as if Nature had stopped to listen too.

The camp rose to its feet as one man! It was proposed to explode a barrel of gunpowder; but in consideration of the situation of the mother, better counsels prevailed, and only a few revolvers were discharged; for whether owing to the rude surgery of the camp, or some other reason, Cherokee Sal was sinking fast. Within an hour she had climbed, as it were, that rugged road that led to the stars, and so passed out of Roaring Camp, its sin and shame, forever. I do not think that the announcement disturbed them much, except in speculation as to the fate of the child. "Can he live now?" was asked of Stumpy. The answer was doubtful. The only other being of Cherokee Sal's sex and maternal condition in the settlement was an ass. There was some conjecture as to fitness, but the experiment was tried. It was less problematical than the ancient treatment of Romulus and Remus, and apparently as successful.

When these details were completed, which exhausted another hour, the door was opened, and the anxious crowd of men, who had already formed themselves into a queue, entered in single file. Beside the low bunk or shelf, on which the figure of the mother was starkly outlined below the blankets, stood a pine table. On this a candle-box was placed, and within it, swathed in staring red flannel, lay the last arrival at Roaring Camp. Beside the candle-box was placed a hat. Its use was soon indicated. "Gentlemen," said Stumpy, with a singular mixture of authority and *ex officio* complacency, — "gentlemen will please pass in at the front door, round the table, and out at the back door. Them as wishes to contribute anything toward the orphan will find a hat handy." The first man entered with his hat on; he uncovered, however, as he looked about him, and so unconsciously set an example to the next. In such communities good and bad actions are catching. As the procession filed in comments were audible, — criticisms addressed perhaps rather to Stumpy in the character of showman: "Is that him?" "Mighty small specimen;" "Has n't more 'n got the color;" "Ain't bigger nor a derringer." The contributions were as characteristic: A silver tobacco box; a doubloon; a navy revolver, silver mounted; a gold specimen; a very beautifully embroidered lady's handkerchief (from Oakhurst the gambler); a diamond breastpin; a diamond ring (suggested by the pin, with the remark from the giver that he "saw that pin and went two diamonds better"); a slung-shot; a Bible (contributor not detected); a golden spur; a silver teaspoon (the initials, I regret to say, were not the giver's); a pair of surgeon's shears; a lancet; a Bank of England note for £5; and about $200 in loose gold and silver coin. During these proceedings Stumpy maintained a silence as impassive as the dead on his left, a gravity as inscrutable as that of the newly born on his right. Only one incident occurred to break the monotony of the curious procession. As Kentuck bent over the candle-box half curiously, the child turned, and, in a spasm of pain, caught at his groping finger, and held it fast for a moment. Kentuck looked foolish and embarrassed. Something like a blush tried to assert itself in his weather-beaten cheek. "The d—d little cuss!" he said, as he extricated his finger, with perhaps more tenderness and care than he might have been deemed capable of showing. He held that finger a little apart from its fellows as he went out, and examined it curiously. The examination provoked the same original remark in regard to the child. In fact, he seemed to enjoy repeating it. "He rastled with my finger," he remarked to Tipton, holding up the member, "the d—d little cuss!"

It was four o'clock before the camp sought repose. A light burnt in the cabin where the watchers sat, for Stumpy did not go to bed that night. Nor did Kentuck. He drank quite freely, and related with great gusto his experience, invariably ending with his characteristic condemnation of the newcomer. It seemed to relieve him of any unjust implication of sentiment, and Kentuck had the weaknesses of the nobler sex. When everybody else had gone to bed, he walked down to the river and whistled reflectingly. Then he walked up the gulch past the cabin, still whistling with demonstrative unconcern. At a large redwood-tree he paused and retraced his steps, and again passed the cabin. Halfway down to the river's bank he again paused, and then returned and knocked at the door. It was opened by Stumpy. "How goes it?" said Kentuck, looking past Stumpy toward the candle-box. "All serene!" replied Stumpy. "Anything up?" "Nothing." There was a pause — an embarrassing one — Stumpy still holding the door. Then Kentuck had recourse to his finger, which he held up to Stumpy. "Rastled with it, — the d—d little cuss," he said, and retired.

The next day Cherokee Sal had such rude sepulture as Roaring Camp afforded. After her body had been committed to the hillside, there was a formal meeting of the camp to discuss what should be done with her infant. A resolution to adopt it was unanimous and enthusiastic. But an animated discussion in regard to the manner and feasibility of providing for its wants at once sprang up. It was remarkable that the argument partook of none of those fierce personalities with which discussions were usually conducted at Roaring Camp. Tipton proposed that they should send the child to Red Dog, — a distance of forty miles, — where female attention could be procured. But the unlucky suggestion met with fierce and unanimous opposition. It was evident that no plan which entailed parting from their new acquisition would for a moment be entertained. "Besides," said Tom Ryder, "them fellows at Red Dog would swap it, and ring in somebody else on us." A disbelief in the honesty of other camps prevailed at Roaring Camp, as in other places.

The introduction of a female nurse in the camp also met with objection. It was argued that no decent woman could be prevailed to accept Roaring Camp as her home, and the speaker urged that "they did n't want any more of the other kind." This unkind allusion to the defunct mother, harsh as it may seem, was the first spasm of propriety, — the first symptom of the camp's regeneration. Stumpy advanced nothing. Perhaps he felt a certain delicacy in interfering with the selection of a possible successor in office. But when questioned, he averred stoutly that he and "Jinny" — the mammal before alluded to — could manage to rear the child. There was something original, independent, and heroic about the plan that pleased the camp. Stumpy was retained. Certain articles were sent for to Sacramento. "Mind," said the treasurer, as he pressed a bag of gold-dust into the expressman's hand, "the best that can be got, — lace, you know, and filigree-work and frills, — d—n the cost!"

Strange to say, the child thrived. Perhaps the invigorating climate of the mountain camp was compensation for material deficiencies. Nature took the foundling to her broader breast. In that rare atmosphere of the Sierra foothills, — that air pungent with balsamic odor, that ethereal cordial at once bracing and exhilarating, — he may have found food and nourishment, or a subtle chemistry that transmuted ass's milk to lime and phosphorus. Stumpy inclined to the belief that it was the latter and good nursing. "Me and that ass," he would say, "has been father and mother to him! Don't you," he would add, apostrophizing the helpless bundle before him, "never go back on us."

By the time he was a month old the necessity of giving him a name became apparent. He had generally been known as "The Kid," "Stumpy's Boy," "The Coyote" (an allusion to his vocal powers), and even by Kentuck's endearing diminutive of "The d—d little cuss." But these were felt to be vague and unsatisfactory, and were at last dismissed under another influence. Gamblers and adventurers are generally superstitious, and Oakhurst one day declared that the baby had brought "the luck" to Roaring Camp. It was certain that of late they had been successful. "Luck" was the name agreed upon, with the prefix of Tommy for greater convenience. No allusion was made to the mother, and the father was unknown. "It's better," said the philosophical Oakhurst, "to take a fresh deal all round. Call him Luck, and start him fair." A day was accordingly set apart for the christening. What was meant by this ceremony the reader may imagine who has already gathered some idea of the reckless irreverence of Roaring Camp. The master of ceremonies was one "Boston," a noted wag, and the occasion seemed to promise the greatest facetiousness. This ingenious satirist had spent two days in preparing a burlesque of the Church service, with pointed local allusions. The choir was properly trained, and Sandy Tipton was to stand godfather. But after the procession had marched to the grove with music and banners, and the child had been deposited before a mock altar, Stumpy stepped before the expectant crowd. "It ain't my style to spoil fun, boys," said the little man, stoutly eying the faces around him, "but it strikes me that this thing ain't exactly on the squar. It's playing it pretty low down on this yer baby to ring in fun on him that he ain't goin' to understand. And ef there's goin' to be any godfathers round, I'd like to see who's got any better rights than me." A silence followed Stumpy's speech. To the credit of all humorists be it said that the first man to acknowledge its justice was the satirist thus stopped of his fun. "But," said Stumpy, quickly following up his advantage, "we're here for a christening, and we'll have it. I proclaim you Thomas Luck, according to the laws of the United States and the State of California, so help me God." It was the first time that the name of the Deity had been otherwise uttered than profanely in the camp. The form of christening was perhaps even more ludicrous than the satirist had conceived; but strangely enough, nobody saw it and nobody laughed. "Tommy" was christened as seriously as he would have been under a Christian roof, and cried and was comforted in as orthodox fashion.

And so the work of regeneration began in Roaring Camp. Almost imperceptibly a change came over the settlement. The cabin assigned to "Tommy Luck" — or "The Luck," as he was more frequently called — first showed signs of improvement. It was kept scrupulously clean and whitewashed. Then it was boarded, clothed, and papered. The rosewood cradle, packed eighty miles by mule, had, in Stumpy's way of putting it, "sorter killed the rest of the furniture." So the rehabilitation of the cabin became a necessity. The men who were in the habit of lounging in at Stumpy's to see "how 'The Luck' got on" seemed to appreciate the change, and in self-defense the rival establishment of "Tuttle's grocery" bestirred itself and imported a carpet and mirrors. The reflections of the latter on the appearance of Roaring Camp tended to produce stricter habits of personal cleanliness. Again Stumpy imposed a kind of quarantine upon those who aspired to the honor and privilege of holding The Luck. It was a cruel mortification to Kentuck — who, in the carelessness of a large nature and the habits of frontier life, had begun to regard all garments as a second cuticle, which, like a snake's, only sloughed off through decay — to be debarred this privilege from certain prudential reasons. Yet such was the subtle influence of innovation that he thereafter appeared regularly every afternoon in a clean shirt and face still shining from his ablutions. Nor were moral and social sanitary laws neglected. "Tommy," who was supposed to spend his whole existence in a persistent attempt to repose, must not be disturbed by noise. The shouting and yelling, which had gained the camp its infelicitous title, were not permitted within hearing distance of Stumpy's. The men conversed in whispers or smoked with Indian gravity. Profanity was tacitly given up in these sacred pre cincts, and throughout the camp a popular form of expletive, known as "D—n the luck!" and "Curse the luck!" was abandoned, as having a new personal bearing. Vocal music was not interdicted, being supposed to have a soothing, tranquilizing quality; and one song, sung by "Man-o'-War Jack," an English sailor from her Majesty's Australian colonies, was quite popular as a lullaby. It was a lugubrious recital of the exploits of "the Arethusa, Seventy-four," in a muffled minor, ending with a prolonged dying fall at the burden of each verse, "On b-oo-o-ard of the Arethusa." It was a fine sight to see Jack holding The Luck, rocking from side to side as if with the motion of a ship, and crooning forth this naval ditty. Either through the peculiar rocking of Jack or the length of his song, — it contained ninety stanzas, and was continued with conscientious deliberation to the bitter end, — the lullaby generally had the desired effect. At such times the men would lie at full length under the trees in the soft summer twilight, smoking their pipes and drinking in the melodious utterances. An indistinct idea that this was pastoral happiness pervaded the camp. "This 'ere kind o' think," said the Cockney Simmons, meditatively reclining on his elbow, "is 'evingly." It reminded him of Greenwich.

On the long summer days The Luck was usually carried to the gulch from whence the golden store of Roaring Camp was taken. There, on a blanket spread over pine boughs, he would lie while the men were working in the ditches below. Latterly there was a rude attempt to decorate this bower with flowers and sweet-smelling shrubs, and generally some one would bring him a cluster of wild honeysuckles, azaleas, or the painted blossoms of Las Mariposas. The men had suddenly awakened to the fact that there were beauty and significance in these trifles, which they had so long trodden carelessly beneath their feet. A flake of glittering mica, a fragment of variegated quartz, a bright pebble from the bed of the creek, became beautiful to eyes thus cleared and strengthened, and were invariably put aside for The Luck. It was wonderful how many treasures the woods and hillsides yielded that "would do for Tommy." Surrounded by playthings such as never child out of fairyland had before, it is to be hoped that Tommy was content. He appeared to be serenely happy, albeit there was an infantine gravity about him, a contemplative light in his round gray eyes, that sometimes worried Stumpy. He was always tractable and quiet, and it is recorded that once, having crept beyond his "corral," — a hedge of tessellated pine boughs, which surrounded his bed, — he dropped over the bank on his head in the soft earth, and remained with his mottled legs in the air in that position for at least five minutes with unflinching gravity. He was extricated without a murmur. I hesitate to record the many other instances of his sagacity, which rest, unfortunately, upon the statements of prejudiced friends. Some of them were not without a tinge of superstition. "I crep' up the bank just now," said Kentuck one day, in a breathless state of excitement, "and dern my skin if he was n't a-talking to a jaybird as was a-sittin' on his lap. There they was, just as free and sociable as anything you please, a-jawin' at each other just like two cherrybums." Howbeit, whether creeping over the pine boughs or lying lazily on his back blinking at the leaves above him, to him the birds sang, the squirrels chattered, and the flowers bloomed. Nature was his nurse and playfellow. For him she would let slip between the leaves golden shafts of sunlight that fell just within his grasp; she would send wandering breezes to visit him with the balm of bay and resinous gum; to him the tall redwoods nodded familiarly and sleepily, the bumblebees buzzed, and the rooks cawed a slumbrous accompaniment.

Such was the golden summer of Roaring Camp. They

were "flush times," and the luck was with them. The claims had yielded enormously. The camp was jealous of its privileges and looked suspiciously on strangers. No encouragement was given to immigration, and, to make their seclusion more perfect, the land on either side of the mountain wall that surrounded the camp they duly preëmpted. This, and a reputation for singular proficiency with the revolver, kept the reserve of Roaring Camp inviolate. The expressman — their only connecting link with the surrounding world — sometimes told wonderful stories of the camp. He would say, "They 've a street up there in 'Roaring' that would lay over any street in Red Dog. They 've got vines and flowers round their houses, and they wash themselves twice a day. But they 're mighty rough on strangers, and they worship an Ingin baby."

With the prosperity of the camp came a desire for further improvement. It was proposed to build a hotel in the following spring, and to invite one or two decent families to reside there for the sake of The Luck, who might perhaps profit by female companionship. The sacrifice that this concession to the sex cost these men, who were fiercely skeptical in regard to its general virtue and usefulness, can only be accounted for by their affection for Tommy. A few still held out. But the resolve could not be carried into effect for three months, and the minority meekly yielded in the hope that something might turn up to prevent it. And it did.

The winter of 1851 will long be remembered in the foothills. The snow lay deep on the Sierras, and every mountain creek became a river, and every river a lake. Each gorge and gulch was transformed into a tumultuous watercourse that descended the hillsides, tearing down giant trees and scattering its drift and débris along the plain. Red Dog had been twice under water, and Roaring Camp had been forewarned. "Water put the gold into them gulches," said Stumpy. "It 's been here once and will be here again!" And that night the North Fork suddenly leaped over its banks and swept up the triangular valley of Roaring Camp.

In the confusion of rushing water, crashing trees, and crackling timber, and the darkness which seemed to flow with the water and blot out the fair valley, but little could be done to collect the scattered camp. When the morning broke, the cabin of Stumpy, nearest the river-bank, was gone. Higher up the gulch they found the body of its unlucky owner; but the pride, the hope, the joy, The Luck, of Roaring Camp had disappeared. They were returning with sad hearts when a shout from the bank recalled them.

It was a relief-boat from down the river. They had picked up, they said, a man and an infant, nearly exhausted, about two miles below. Did anybody know them, and did they belong here?

It needed but a glance to show them Kentuck lying there, cruelly crushed and bruised, but still holding The Luck of Roaring Camp in his arms. As they bent over the strangely assorted pair, they saw that the child was cold and pulseless. "He is dead," said one. Kentuck opened his eyes. "Dead?" he repeated feebly. "Yes, my man, and you are dying too." A smile lit the eyes of the expiring Kentuck. "Dying!" he repeated; "he 's a-taking me with him. Tell the boys I 've got The Luck with me now;" and the strong man, clinging to the frail babe as a drowning man is said to cling to a straw, drifted away into the shadowy river that flows forever to the unknown sea.

# THE OUTCASTS OF POKER FLAT

As Mr. John Oakhurst, gambler, stepped into the main street of Poker Flat on the morning of the 23d of November, 1850, he was conscious of a change in its moral atmosphere since the preceding night. Two or three men, conversing earnestly together, ceased as he approached, and exchanged significant glances. There was a Sabbath lull in the air, which, in a settlement unused to Sabbath influences, looked ominous.

Mr. Oakhurst's calm, handsome face betrayed small concern in these indications. Whether he was conscious of any predisposing cause was another question. "I reckon they 're after somebody," he reflected; "likely it 's me." He returned to his pocket the handkerchief with which he had been whipping away the red dust of Poker Flat from his neat boots, and quietly discharged his mind of any further conjecture.

In point of fact, Poker Flat was "after somebody." It had lately suffered the loss of several thousand dollars, two valuable horses, and a prominent citizen. It was experiencing a spasm of virtuous reaction, quite as lawless and ungovernable as any of the acts that had provoked it. A secret committee had determined to rid the town of all improper persons. This was done permanently in regard of two men who were then hanging from the boughs of a sycamore in the gulch, and temporarily in the banishment of certain other objectionable characters. I regret to say that some of these were ladies. It is but due to the sex, however, to state that their impropriety was professional, and it was only in such easily established standards of evil that Poker Flat ventured to sit in judgment.

Mr. Oakhurst was right in supposing that he was included in this category. A few of the committee had urged hanging him as a possible example and a sure method of reimbursing themselves from his pockets of the sums he had won from them. "It 's agin justice," said Jim Wheeler, "to let this yer young man from Roaring Camp — an entire stranger — carry away our money." But a crude sentiment of equity residing in the breasts of those who had been fortunate enough to win from Mr. Oakhurst overruled this narrower local prejudice.

Mr. Oakhurst received his sentence with philosophic calmness, none the less coolly that he was aware of the hesitation of his judges. He was too much of a gambler not to accept fate. With him life was at best an uncertain game, and he recognized the usual percentage in favor of the dealer.

A body of armed men accompanied the deported wickedness of Poker Flat to the outskirts of the settlement. Besides Mr. Oakhurst, who was known to be a coolly desperate man, and for whose intimidation the armed escort was intended, the expatriated party consisted of a young woman familiarly known as "The Duchess;" another who had won the title of "Mother Shipton;" and "Uncle Billy," a suspected sluice-robber and confirmed drunkard. The cavalcade provoked no comments from the spectators, nor was any word uttered by the escort. Only when the gulch which marked the uttermost limit of Poker Flat was reached, the leader spoke briefly and to the point. The exiles were forbidden to return at the peril of their lives.

As the escort disappeared, their pent-up feelings found vent in a few hysterical tears from the Duchess, some bad language from Mother Shipton, and a Parthian volley of expletives from Uncle Billy. The philosophic Oakhurst alone remained silent. He listened calmly to Mother Shipton's desire to cut somebody's heart out, to the repeated statements of the Duchess that she would die in the road, and to the alarming oaths that seemed to be bumped out of Uncle Billy as he rode forward. With the easy good humor characteristic of his class, he insisted upon exchanging his own riding-horse, "Five-Spot," for the sorry mule which the Duchess rode. But even this act did not draw the party into any closer sympathy. The young woman readjusted her somewhat draggled plumes with a feeble, faded coquetry; Mother Shipton eyed the possessor of "Five-Spot" with malevolence, and Uncle Billy included the whole party in one sweeping anathema.

The road to Sandy Bar — a camp that, not having as yet experienced the regenerating influences of Poker Flat, consequently seemed to offer some invitation to the emigrants — lay over a steep mountain range. It was distant a day's severe travel. In that advanced season the party soon passed out of the moist, temperate regions of the foothills into the dry, cold, bracing air of the Sierras. The trail was narrow and difficult. At noon the Duchess, rolling out of her saddle upon the ground, declared her intention of going no farther, and the party halted.

The spot was singularly wild and impressive. A wooded amphitheatre, surrounded on three sides by precipitous cliffs of naked granite, sloped gently toward the crest of another precipice that overlooked the valley. It was, undoubtedly, the most suitable spot for a camp, had camping been advisable. But Mr. Oakhurst knew that scarcely half the journey to Sandy Bar was accomplished, and the party were not equipped or provisioned for delay. This fact he pointed out to his companions curtly, with a philosophic commentary on the folly of "throwing up their hand before the game was played out." But they were furnished with liquor, which in this emergency stood them in place of food, fuel, rest, and prescience. In spite of his remonstrances, it was not long before they were more or less under its influence. Uncle Billy passed rapidly from a bellicose state into one of stupor, the Duchess became maudlin, and Mother Shipton snored. Mr. Oakhurst alone remained erect, leaning against a rock, calmly surveying them.

Mr. Oakhurst did not drink. It interfered with a profession which required coolness, impassiveness, and presence of mind, and, in his own language, he "could n't afford it." As he gazed at his recumbent fellow exiles, the loneliness begotten of his pariah trade, his habits of life, his very vices, for the first time seriously oppressed him. He bestirred himself in dusting his black clothes, washing his hands and face, and other acts characteristic of his studiously neat habits, and for a moment forgot his annoyance. The thought of deserting his weaker and more pitiable companions never perhaps occurred to him. Yet he could not help feeling the want of that excitement which, singularly enough, was most conducive to that calm equanimity for which he was notorious. He looked at the gloomy walls that rose a thousand feet sheer above the circling pines around him, at the sky ominously clouded, at the valley below, already deepening into shadow; and, doing so, suddenly he heard his own name called.

A horseman slowly ascended the trail. In the fresh, open face of the newcomer Mr. Oakhurst recognized Tom Simson, otherwise known as "The Innocent," of Sandy Bar. He had met him some months before over a "little game," and had, with perfect equanimity, won the entire fortune — amounting to some forty dollars — of that guileless youth. After the game was finished, Mr. Oakhurst drew the youthful speculator behind the door and thus addressed him: "Tommy, you 're a good little man, but you can't gamble worth a cent. Don't try it over again." He then handed him his money back, pushed him gently from the room, and so made a devoted slave of Tom Simson.

There was a remembrance of this in his boyish and enthusiastic greeting of Mr. Oakhurst. He had started, he said, to go to Poker Flat to seek his fortune. "Alone?" No, not exactly alone; in fact (a giggle), he had run away with Piney Woods. Did n't Mr. Oakhurst remember Piney? She that used to wait on the table at the Temperance House? They had been engaged a long time, but old Jake Woods had objected, and so they had run away, and were going to Poker Flat to be married, and here they were. And they were tired out, and how lucky it was they had found a place to camp, and company. All this the Innocent delivered rapidly, while Piney, a stout, comely damsel of fifteen, emerged from behind the pine-tree, where she had been blushing unseen, and rode to the side of her lover.

Mr. Oakhurst seldom troubled himself with sentiment, still less with propriety; but he had a vague idea that the situation was not fortunate. He retained, however, his presence of mind sufficiently to kick Uncle Billy, who was about to say something, and Uncle Billy was sober enough to recognize in Mr. Oakhurst's kick a superior power that would not bear trifling. He then endeavored to dissuade Tom Simson from delaying further, but in vain. He even pointed out the fact that there was no provision, nor means of making a camp. But, unluckily, the Innocent met this objection by assuring the party that he was provided with an extra mule loaded with provisions, and by the discovery of a rude attempt at a log house near the trail. "Piney can stay with Mrs. Oakhurst," said the Innocent, pointing to the Duchess, "and I can shift for myself."

Nothing but Mr. Oakhurst's admonishing foot saved Uncle Billy from bursting into a roar of laughter. As it was, he felt compelled to retire up the cañon until he could recover his gravity. There he confided the joke to the tall pine-trees, with many slaps of his leg, contortions of his face, and the usual profanity. But when he returned to the party, he found them seated by a fire — for the air had grown strangely chill and the sky overcast — in apparently amicable conversation. Piney was actually talking in an impulsive girlish fashion to the Duchess, who was listening with an interest and animation she had not shown for many days. The Innocent was holding forth, apparently with equal effect, to Mr. Oakhurst and Mother Shipton, who was actually relaxing into amiability. "Is this yer a d—d picnic?" said Uncle Billy, with inward scorn, as he surveyed the sylvan group, the glancing firelight, and the tethered animals in the foreground. Suddenly an idea mingled with the alcoholic fumes that disturbed his brain. It was apparently of a jocular nature, for he felt impelled to slap his leg again and cram his fist into his mouth.

As the shadows crept slowly up the mountain, a slight breeze rocked the tops of the pine-trees and moaned through their long and gloomy aisles. The ruined cabin, patched and covered with pine boughs, was set apart for the ladies. As the lovers parted, they unaffectedly exchanged a kiss, so honest and sincere that it might have been heard above the swaying pines. The frail Duchess and the malevolent Mother Shipton were probably too stunned to remark upon this last evidence of simplicity, and so turned without a word to the hut. The fire was replenished, the men lay down before the door, and in a few minutes were asleep.

Mr. Oakhurst was a light sleeper. Toward morning he awoke benumbed and cold. As he stirred the dying fire, the wind, which was now blowing strongly, brought to his cheek that which caused the blood to leave it, — snow!

He started to his feet with the intention of awakening

the sleepers, for there was no time to lose. But turning to where Uncle Billy had been lying, he found him gone. A suspicion leaped to his brain, and a curse to his lips. He ran to the spot where the mules had been tethered — they were no longer there. The tracks were already rapidly disappearing in the snow.

The momentary excitement brought Mr. Oakhurst back to the fire with his usual calm. He did not waken the sleepers. The Innocent slumbered peacefully, with a smile on his good-humored, freckled face; the virgin Piney slept beside her frailer sisters as sweetly as though attended by celestial guardians; and Mr. Oakhurst, drawing his blanket over his shoulders, stroked his mustaches and waited for the dawn. It came slowly in a whirling mist of snowflakes that dazzled and confused the eye. What could be seen of the landscape appeared magically changed. He looked over the valley, and summed up the present and future in two words, "Snowed in!"

A careful inventory of the provisions, which, fortunately for the party, had been stored within the hut, and so escaped the felonious fingers of Uncle Billy, disclosed the fact that with care and prudence they might last ten days longer. "That is," said Mr. Oakhurst *sotto voce* to the Innocent, "if you 're willing to board us. If you ain't — and perhaps you 'd better not — you can wait till Uncle Billy gets back with provisions." For some occult reason, Mr. Oakhurst could not bring himself to disclose Uncle Billy's rascality, and so offered the hypothesis that he had wandered from the camp and had accidentally stampeded the animals. He dropped a warning to the Duchess and Mother Shipton, who of course knew the facts of their associate's defection. "They 'll find out the truth about us *all* when they find out anything," he added significantly, "and there 's no good frightening them now."

Tom Simson not only put all his worldly store at the

disposal of Mr. Oakhurst, but seemed to enjoy the prospect of their enforced seclusion. "We 'll have a good camp for a week, and then the snow 'll melt, and we 'll all go back together." The cheerful gayety of the young man and Mr. Oakhurst's calm infected the others. The Innocent, with the aid of pine boughs, extemporized a thatch for the roofless cabin, and the Duchess directed Piney in the rearrangement of the interior with a taste and tact that opened the blue eyes of that provincial maiden to their fullest extent. "I reckon now you 're used to fine things at Poker Flat," said Piney. The Duchess turned away sharply to conceal something that reddened her cheeks through their professional tint, and Mother Shipton requested Piney not to "chatter." But when Mr. Oakhurst returned from a weary search for the trail, he heard the sound of happy laughter echoed from the rocks. He stopped in some alarm, and his thoughts first naturally reverted to the whiskey, which he had prudently cachéd. "And yet it don't somehow sound like whiskey," said the gambler. It was not until he caught sight of the blazing fire through the still blinding storm, and the group around it, that he settled to the conviction that it was "square fun."

Whether Mr. Oakhurst had cachéd his cards with the whiskey as something debarred the free access of the community, I cannot say. It was certain that, in Mother Shipton's words, he "did n't say 'cards' once" during that evening. Haply the time was beguiled by an accordion, produced somewhat ostentatiously by Tom Simson from his pack. Notwithstanding some difficulties attending the manipulation of this instrument, Piney Woods managed to pluck several reluctant melodies from its keys, to an accompaniment by the Innocent on a pair of bone castanets. But the crowning festivity of the evening was reached in a rude camp-meeting hymn, which the lovers, joining hands, sang with great earnestness and vociferation. I fear that a certain defiant tone and Covenanter's swing to its chorus, rather than any devotional quality, caused it speedily to infect the others, who at last joined in the refrain: —

> "I 'm proud to live in the service of the Lord,
> And I 'm bound to die in His army."

The pines rocked, the storm eddied and whirled above the miserable group, and the flames of their altar leaped heavenward, as if in token of the vow.

At midnight the storm abated, the rolling clouds parted, and the stars glittered keenly above the sleeping camp. Mr. Oakhurst, whose professional habits had enabled him to live on the smallest possible amount of sleep, in dividing the watch with Tom Simson somehow managed to take upon himself the greater part of that duty. He excused himself to the Innocent by saying that he had "often been a week without sleep." "Doing what?" asked Tom. "Poker!" replied Oakhurst sententiously. "When a man gets a streak of luck, — nigger-luck, — he don't get tired. The luck gives in first. Luck," continued the gambler reflectively, "is a mighty queer thing. All you know about it for certain is that it 's bound to change. And it 's finding out when it 's going to change that makes you. We 've had a streak of bad luck since we left Poker Flat, — you come along, and slap you get into it, too. If you can hold your cards right along you 're all right. For," added the gambler, with cheerful irrelevance —

> "'I 'm proud to live in the service of the Lord,
> And I 'm bound to die in His army.'"

The third day came, and the sun, looking through the white-curtained valley, saw the outcasts divide their slowly decreasing store of provisions for the morning meal. It was one of the peculiarities of that mountain climate that its rays diffused a kindly warmth over the wintry landscape, as if in regretful commiseration of the past. But it revealed drift on drift of snow piled high around the hut, — a hopeless, uncharted, trackless sea of white lying below the rocky shores to which the castaways still clung. Through the marvelously clear air the smoke of the pastoral village of Poker Flat rose miles away. Mother Shipton saw it, and from a remote pinnacle of her rocky fastness hurled in that direction a final malediction. It was her last vituperative attempt, and perhaps for that reason was invested with a certain degree of sublimity. It did her good, she privately informed the Duchess. "Just you go out there and cuss, and see." She then set herself to the task of amusing "the child," as she and the Duchess were pleased to call Piney. Piney was no chicken, but it was a soothing and original theory of the pair thus to account for the fact that she did n't swear and was n't improper.

When night crept up again through the gorges, the reedy notes of the accordion rose and fell in fitful spasms and long-drawn gasps by the flickering campfire. But music failed to fill entirely the aching void left by insufficient food, and a new diversion was proposed by Piney, — story-telling. Neither Mr. Oakhurst nor his female companions caring to relate their personal experiences, this plan would have failed too, but for the Innocent. Some months before he had chanced upon a stray copy of Mr. Pope's ingenious translation of the Iliad. He now proposed to narrate the principal incidents of that poem — having thoroughly mastered the argument and fairly forgotten the words — in the current vernacular of Sandy Bar. And so for the rest of that night the Homeric demigods again walked the earth. Trojan bully and wily Greek wrestled in the winds, and the great pines in the cañon seemed to bow to the wrath of the son of Peleus. Mr. Oakhurst listened with quiet satisfaction. Most especially was he interested in the fate of "Ash-heels," as the Innocent persisted in denominating the "swift-footed Achilles."

So, with small food and much of Homer and the accordion, a week passed over the heads of the outcasts. The sun again forsook them, and again from leaden skies the snowflakes were sifted over the land. Day by day closer around them drew the snowy circle, until at last they looked from their prison over drifted walls of dazzling white, that towered twenty feet above their heads. It became more and more difficult to replenish their fires, even from the fallen trees beside them, now half hidden in the drifts. And yet no one complained. The lovers turned from the dreary prospect and looked into each other's eyes, and were happy. Mr. Oakhurst settled himself coolly to the losing game before him. The Duchess, more cheerful than she had been, assumed the care of Piney. Only Mother Shipton — once the strongest of the party — seemed to sicken and fade. At midnight on the tenth day she called Oakhurst to her side. "I 'm going," she said, in a voice of querulous weakness, "but don't say anything about it. Don't waken the kids. Take the bundle from under my head, and open it." Mr. Oakhurst did so. It contained Mother Shipton's rations for the last week, untouched. "Give 'em to the child," she said, pointing to the sleeping Piney. "You 've starved yourself," said the gambler. "That 's what they call it," said the woman querulously, as she lay down again, and, turning her face to the wall, passed quietly away.

The accordion and the bones were put aside that day, and Homer was forgotten. When the body of Mother Shipton had been committed to the snow, Mr. Oakhurst took the Innocent aside, and showed him a pair of snowshoes, which he had fashioned from the old pack-saddle. "There 's one chance in a hundred to save her yet," he said, pointing to Piney; "but it 's there," he added, pointing toward Poker Flat. "If you can reach there in two days she 's safe." "And you ?" asked Tom Simson. "I 'll stay here," was the curt reply.

The lovers parted with a long embrace. "You are not going, too?" said the Duchess, as she saw Mr. Oakhurst apparently waiting to accompany him. "As far as the cañon," he replied. He turned suddenly and kissed the Duchess, leaving her pallid face aflame, and her trembling limbs rigid with amazement.

Night came, but not Mr. Oakhurst. It brought the storm again and the whirling snow. Then the Duchess, feeding the fire, found that some one had quietly piled beside the hut enough fuel to last a few days longer. The tears rose to her eyes, but she hid them from Piney.

The women slept but little. In the morning, looking into each other's faces, they read their fate. Neither spoke, but Piney, accepting the position of the stronger, drew near and placed her arm around the Duchess's waist. They kept this attitude for the rest of the day. That night the storm reached its greatest fury, and, rending asunder the protecting vines, invaded the very hut.

Toward morning they found themselves unable to feed the fire, which gradually died away. As the embers slowly blackened, the Duchess crept closer to Piney, and broke the silence of many hours: "Piney, can you pray?" "No, dear," said Piney simply. The Duchess, without knowing exactly why, felt relieved, and, putting her head upon Piney's shoulder, spoke no more. And so reclining, the younger and purer pillowing the head of her soiled sister upon her virgin breast, they fell asleep.

The wind lulled as if it feared to waken them. Feathery drifts of snow, shaken from the long pine boughs, flew like white winged birds, and settled about them as they slept. The moon through the rifted clouds looked down upon what had been the camp. But all human stain, all trace of earthly travail, was hidden beneath the spotless mantle mercifully flung from above.

They slept all that day and the next, nor did they waken

when voices and footsteps broke the silence of the camp. And when pitying fingers brushed the snow from their wan faces, you could scarcely have told from the equal peace that dwelt upon them which was she that had sinned. Even the law of Poker Flat recognized this, and turned away, leaving them still locked in each other's arms.

But at the head of the gulch, on one of the largest pine-trees, they found the deuce of clubs pinned to the bark with a bowie-knife. It bore the following, written in pencil in a firm hand: —

†

BENEATH THIS TREE
LIES THE BODY
OF
JOHN OAKHURST,
WHO STRUCK A STREAK OF BAD LUCK
ON THE 23D OF NOVEMBER 1850,
AND
HANDED IN HIS CHECKS
ON THE 7TH DECEMBER, 1850.

†

And pulseless and cold, with a Derringer by his side and a bullet in his heart, though still calm as in life, beneath the snow lay he who was at once the strongest and yet the weakest of the outcasts of Poker Flat.

## TENNESSEE'S PARTNER

I DO not think that we ever knew his real name. Our ignorance of it certainly never gave us any social inconvenience, for at Sandy Bar in 1854 most men were christened anew. Sometimes these appellatives were derived from some distinctiveness of dress, as in the case of "Dungaree Jack"; or from some peculiarity of habit, as shown in "Saleratus Bill," so called from an undue proportion of that chemical in his daily bread; or from some unlucky slip, as exhibited in "The Iron Pirate," a mild, inoffensive man, who earned that baleful title by his unfortunate mispronunciation of the term "iron pyrites." Perhaps this may have been the beginning of a rude heraldry; but I am constrained to think that it was because a man's real name in that day rested solely upon his own unsupported statement. "Call yourself Clifford, do you?" said Boston, addressing a timid newcomer with infinite scorn; "hell is full of such Cliffords!" He then introduced the unfortunate man, whose name happened to be really Clifford, as "Jaybird Charley," — an unhallowed inspiration of the moment that clung to him ever after.

But to return to Tennessee's Partner, whom we never knew by any other than this relative title. That he had ever existed as a separate and distinct individuality we only learned later. It seems that in 1853 he left Poker Flat to go to San Francisco, ostensibly to procure a wife. He never got any farther than Stockton. At that place he was attracted by a young person who waited upon the table at the hotel where he took his meals. One morning he said something to her which caused her to smile not unkindly, to somewhat coquettishly break a plate of toast over his upturned, serious, simple face, and to retreat to the kitchen. He followed her, and emerged a few moments later, covered with more toast and victory. That day week they were married by a justice of the peace, and returned to Poker Flat. I am aware that something more might be made of this episode, but I prefer to tell it as it was current at Sandy Bar, — in the gulches and bar-rooms, — where all sentiment was modified by a strong sense of humor.

Of their married felicity but little is known, perhaps for the reason that Tennessee, then living with his partner, one day took occasion to say something to the bride on his own account, at which, it is said, she smiled not unkindly and chastely retreated, — this time as far as Marysville, where Tennessee followed her, and where they went to housekeeping without the aid of a justice of the peace. Tennessee's Partner took the loss of his wife simply and seriously, as was his fashion. But to everybody's surprise, when Tennessee one day returned from Marysville, without his partner's wife, — she having smiled and retreated with somebody else, — Tennessee's Partner was the first man to shake his hand and greet him with affection. The boys who had gathered in the cañon to see the shooting were naturally indignant. Their indignation might have found vent in sarcasm but for a certain look in Tennessee's Partner's eye that indicated a lack of humorous appreciation. In fact, he was a grave man, with a steady application to practical detail which was unpleasant in a difficulty.

Meanwhile a popular feeling against Tennessee had grown up on the Bar. He was known to be a gambler; he was suspected to be a thief. In these suspicions Tennessee's Partner was equally compromised; his continued intimacy with Tennessee after the affair above quoted could only be accounted for on the hypothesis of a copartnership of crime. At last Tennessee's guilt became flagrant. One day he overtook a stranger on his way to Red Dog. The stranger afterward related that Tennessee beguiled the time with interesting anecdote and reminiscence, but illogically concluded the interview in the following words: "And now, young man, I 'll trouble you for your knife, your pistols, and your money. You see your weppings might get you into trouble at Red Dog, and your money 's a temptation to the evilly disposed. I think you said your address was San Francisco. I shall endeavor to call." It may be stated here that Tennessee had a fine flow of humor, which no business preoccupation could wholly subdue.

This exploit was his last. Red Dog and Sandy Bar made common cause against the highwayman. Tennessee was hunted in very much the same fashion as his prototype, the grizzly. As the toils closed around him, he made a desperate dash through the Bar, emptying his revolver at the crowd before the Arcade Saloon, and so on up Grizzly Cañon; but at its farther extremity he was stopped by a small man on a gray horse. The men looked at each other a moment in silence. Both were fearless, both self-possessed and independent, and both types of a civilization that in the seventeenth century would have been called heroic, but in the nineteenth simply "reckless."

"What have you got there? — I call," said Tennessee quietly.

"Two bowers and an ace," said the stranger as quietly, showing two revolvers and a bowie-knife.

"That takes me," returned Tennessee; and, with this gambler's epigram, he threw away his useless pistol and rode back with his captor.

It was a warm night. The cool breeze which usually sprang up with the going down of the sun behind the chaparral-crested mountain was that evening withheld from

Sandy Bar. The little cañon was stifling with heated resinous odors, and the decaying driftwood on the Bar sent forth faint sickening exhalations. The feverishness of day and its fierce passions still filled the camp. Lights moved restlessly along the bank of the river, striking no answering reflection from its tawny current. Against the blackness of the pines the windows of the old loft above the express-office stood out staringly bright; and through their curtainless panes the loungers below could see the forms of those who were even then deciding the fate of Tennessee. And above all this, etched on the dark firmament, rose the Sierra, remote and passionless, crowned with remoter passionless stars.

The trial of Tennessee was conducted as fairly as was consistent with a judge and jury who felt themselves to some extent obliged to justify, in their verdict, the previous irregularities of arrest and indictment. The law of Sandy Bar was implacable, but not vengeful. The excitement and personal feeling of the chase were over; with Tennessee safe in their hands, they were ready to listen patiently to any defense, which they were already satisfied was insufficient. There being no doubt in their own minds, they were willing to give the prisoner the benefit of any that might exist. Secure in the hypothesis that he ought to be hanged on general principles, they indulged him with more latitude of defense than his reckless hardihood seemed to ask. The Judge appeared to be more anxious than the prisoner, who, otherwise unconcerned, evidently took a grim pleasure in the responsibility he had created. "I don't take any hand in this yer game," had been his invariable but good-humored reply to all questions. The Judge — who was also his captor — for a moment vaguely regretted that he had not shot him "on sight" that morning, but presently dismissed this human weakness as unworthy of the judicial mind. Nevertheless, when there was a tap at the door, and it was said that Tennessee's Partner was there on behalf of the prisoner, he was admitted at once without question. Perhaps the younger members of the jury, to whom the proceedings were becoming irksomely thoughtful, hailed him as a relief.

For he was not, certainly, an imposing figure. Short and stout, with a square face, sunburned into a preternatural redness, clad in a loose duck "jumper" and trousers streaked and splashed with red soil, his aspect under any circumstances would have been quaint, and was now even ridiculous. As he stooped to deposit at his feet a heavy carpetbag he was carrying, it became obvious, from partially developed legends and inscriptions, that the material with which his trousers had been patched had been originally intended for a less ambitious covering. Yet he advanced with great gravity, and after shaking the hand of each person in the room with labored cordiality, he wiped his serious perplexed face on a red bandana handkerchief, a shade lighter than his complexion, laid his powerful hand upon the table to steady himself, and thus addressed the Judge: —

"I was passin' by," he began, by way of apology, "and I thought I 'd just step in and see how things was gittin' on with Tennessee thar, — my pardner. It 's a hot night. I disremember any sich weather before on the Bar."

He paused a moment, but nobody volunteering any other meteorological recollection, he again had recourse to his pocket-handkerchief, and for some moments mopped his face diligently.

"Have you anything to say on behalf of the prisoner?" said the Judge finally.

"Thet 's it," said Tennessee's Partner, in a tone of relief. "I come yar as Tennessee's pardner, — knowing him nigh on four year, off and on, wet and dry, in luck and out o' luck. His ways ain't aller my ways, but thar ain't any p'ints in that young man, thar ain't any liveliness as he 's been up to, as I don't know. And you sez to me, sez you, — confidential-like, and between man and man, — sez you, 'Do you know anything in his behalf?' and I sez to you, sez I, — confidential - like, as between man and man, — 'What should a man know of his pardner?'"

"Is this all you have to say?" asked the Judge impatiently, feeling, perhaps, that a dangerous sympathy of humor was beginning to humanize the court.

"Thet 's so," continued Tennessee's Partner. "It ain't for me to say anything agin' him. And now, what 's the case? Here 's Tennessee wants money, wants it bad, and does n't like to ask it of his old pardner. Well, what does Tennessee do? He lays for a stranger, and he fetches that stranger; and you lays for *him*, and you fetches *him*; and the honors is easy. And I put it to you, bein' a fa'r-minded man, and to you, gentlemen all, as fa'r-minded men, ef this is n't so."

"Prisoner," said the Judge, interrupting, "have you any questions to ask this man?"

"No! no!" continued Tennessee's Partner hastily. "I play this yer hand alone. To come down to the bed-rock, it 's just this: Tennessee, thar, has played it pretty rough and expensive-like on a stranger, and on this yer camp. And now, what 's the fair thing? Some would say more, some would say less. Here 's seventeen hundred dollars in coarse gold and a watch, — it 's about all my pile, — and call it square!" And before a hand could be raised to prevent him, he had emptied the contents of the carpetbag upon the table.

For a moment his life was in jeopardy. One or two men sprang to their feet, several hands groped for hidden weapons, and a suggestion to "throw him from the window" was only overridden by a gesture from the Judge. Tennessee laughed. And apparently oblivious of the excitement, Tennessee's Partner improved the opportunity to mop his face again with his handkerchief.

When order was restored, and the man was made to understand, by the use of forcible figures and rhetoric, that Tennessee's offense could not be condoned by money, his face took a more serious and sanguinary hue, and those who were nearest to him noticed that his rough hand trembled slightly on the table. He hesitated a moment as he slowly returned the gold to the carpetbag, as if he had not yet entirely caught the elevated sense of justice which swayed the tribunal, and was perplexed with the belief that he had not offered enough. Then he turned to the Judge, and saying, "This yer is a lone hand, played alone, and without my pardner," he bowed to the jury and was about to withdraw, when the Judge called him back: —

"If you have anything to say to Tennessee, you had better say it now."

For the first time that evening the eyes of the prisoner and his strange advocate met. Tennessee smiled, showed his white teeth, and saying, "Euchred, old man!" held out his hand. Tennessee's Partner took it in his own, and saying, "I just dropped in as I was passin' to see how things was gettin' on," let the hand passively fall, and adding that "it was a warm night," again mopped his face with his handkerchief, and without another word withdrew.

The two men never again met each other alive. For the unparalleled insult of a bribe offered to Judge Lynch — who, whether bigoted, weak, or narrow, was at least incorruptible — firmly fixed in the mind of that mythical personage any wavering determination of Tennessee's fate; and at the break of day he was marched, closely guarded, to meet it at the top of Marley's Hill.

How he met it, how cool he was, how he refused to say anything, how perfect were the arrangements of the committee, were all duly reported, with the addition of a warning moral and example to all future evil-doers, in the "Red Dog Clarion," by its editor, who was present, and to whose vigorous English I cheerfully refer the reader. But the beauty of that midsummer morning, the blessed amity of earth and air and sky, the awakened life of the free woods and hills, the joyous renewal and promise of Nature, and above all, the infinite serenity that thrilled through each, was not reported, as not being a part of the social lesson. And yet, when the weak and foolish deed was done, and a life, with its possibilities and responsibilities, had passed out of the misshapen thing that dangled between earth and sky, the birds sang, the flowers bloomed, the sun shone, as cheerily as before; and possibly the "Red Dog Clarion" was right.

Tennessee's Partner was not in the group that surrounded the ominous tree. But as they turned to disperse, attention was drawn to the singular appearance of a motionless donkey-cart halted at the side of the road. As they approached, they at once recognized the venerable "Jenny" and the two-wheeled cart as the property of Tennessee's Partner, used by him in carrying dirt from his claim; and a few paces distant the owner of the equipage himself, sitting under a buckeye-tree, wiping the perspiration from his glowing face. In answer to an inquiry, he said he had come for the body of the "diseased," "if it was all the same to the committee." He did n't wish to "hurry anything"; he could "wait." He was not working that day; and when the gentlemen were done with the "diseased," he would take him. "Ef thar is any present," he added, in his simple, serious way, "as would care to jine in the fun'l, they kin come." Perhaps it was from a sense of humor, which I have already intimated was a feature of Sandy Bar, — perhaps it was from something even better than that, but two thirds of the loungers accepted the invitation at once.

It was noon when the body of Tennessee was delivered into the hands of his partner. As the cart drew up to the fatal tree, we noticed that it contained a rough oblong box,

— apparently made from a section of sluicing, — and half filled with bark and the tassels of pine. The cart was further decorated with slips of willow and made fragrant with buckeye-blossoms. When the body was deposited in the box, Tennessee's Partner drew over it a piece of tarred canvas, and gravely mounting the narrow seat in front, with his feet upon the shafts, urged the little donkey forward. The equipage moved slowly on, at that decorous pace which was habitual with Jenny even under less solemn circumstances. The men — half curiously, half jestingly, but all good-humoredly — strolled along beside the cart, some in advance, some a little in the rear of the homely catafalque. But whether from the narrowing of the road or some present sense of decorum, as the cart passed on, the company fell to the rear in couples, keeping step, and otherwise assuming the external show of a formal procession. Jack Folinsbee, who had at the outset played a funeral march in dumb show upon an imaginary trombone, desisted from a lack of sympathy and appreciation, — not having, perhaps, your true humorist's capacity to be content with the enjoyment of his own fun.

The way led through Grizzly Cañon, by this time clothed in funereal drapery and shadows. The redwoods, burying their moccasined feet in the red soil, stood in Indian file along the track, trailing an uncouth benediction from their bending boughs upon the passing bier. A hare, surprised into helpless inactivity, sat upright and pulsating in the ferns by the roadside as the cortége went by. Squirrels hastened to gain a secure outlook from higher boughs; and the blue-jays, spreading their wings, fluttered before them like outriders, until the outskirts of Sandy Bar were reached, and the solitary cabin of Tennessee's Partner.

Viewed under more favorable circumstances, it would not have been a cheerful place. The unpicturesque site, the rude and unlovely outlines, the unsavory details, which distinguish the nest-building of the California miner, were all here with the dreariness of decay superadded. A few paces from the cabin there was a rough inclosure, which, in the brief days of Tennessee's Partner's matrimonial felicity, had been used as a garden, but was now overgrown with fern. As we approached it, we were surprised to find that what we had taken for a recent attempt at cultivation was the broken soil about an open grave.

The cart was halted before the inclosure, and rejecting the offers of assistance with the same air of simple self-reliance he had displayed throughout, Tennessee's Partner lifted the rough coffin on his back, and deposited it unaided within the shallow grave. He then nailed down the board which served as a lid, and mounting the little mound of earth beside it, took off his hat and slowly mopped his face with his handkerchief. This the crowd felt was a preliminary to speech, and they disposed themselves variously on stumps and boulders, and sat expectant.

"When a man," began Tennessee's Partner slowly, "has been running free all day, what's the natural thing for him to do? Why, to come home. And if he ain't in a condition to go home, what can his best friend do? Why, bring him home. And here's Tennessee has been running free, and we brings him home from his wandering." He paused and picked up a fragment of quartz, rubbed it thoughtfully on his sleeve, and went on: "It ain't the first time that I've packed him on my back, as you see'd me now. It ain't the first time that I brought him to this yer cabin when he could n't help himself; it ain't the first time that I and Jinny have waited for him on yon hill, and picked him up and so fetched him home, when he could n't speak and did n't know me. And now that it's the last time, why" — he paused and rubbed the quartz gently on his sleeve — "you see it's sort of rough on his pardner. And now, gentlemen," he added abruptly, picking up his long-handled shovel, "the fun'l 's over; and my thanks, and Tennessee's thanks, to you for your trouble."

Resisting any proffers of assistance, he began to fill in the grave, turning his back upon the crowd, that after a few moments' hesitation gradually withdrew. As they crossed the little ridge that hid Sandy Bar from view, some, looking back, thought they could see Tennessee's Partner, his work done, sitting upon the grave, his shovel between his knees, and his face buried in his red bandana handkerchief. But it was argued by others that you could n't tell his face from his handkerchief at that distance, and this point remained undecided.

In the reaction that followed the feverish excitement of that day, Tennessee's Partner was not forgotten. A secret investigation had cleared him of any complicity in Tennessee's guilt, and left only a suspicion of his general sanity. Sandy Bar made a point of calling on him, and proffering various uncouth but well-meant kindnesses. But from that day his rude health and great strength seemed visibly to decline; and when the rainy season fairly set in, and the tiny grass-blades were beginning to peep from the rocky mound above Tennessee's grave, he took to his bed.

One night, when the pines beside the cabin were swaying in the storm and trailing their slender fingers over the roof, and the roar and rush of the swollen river were heard below, Tennessee's Partner lifted his head from the pillow, saying, "It is time to go for Tennessee; I must put Jinny in the cart"; and would have risen from his bed but for the restraint of his attendant. Struggling, he still pursued his singular fancy: "There, now, steady, Jinny, — steady, old girl. How dark it is! Look out for the ruts, — and look out for him, too, old gal. Sometimes, you know, when he 's blind drunk, he drops down right in the trail. Keep on straight up to the pine on the top of the hill. Thar! I told you so! — thar he is, — coming this way, too, — all by himself, sober, and his face a-shining. Tennessee! Pardner!"

And so they met.

## THE ILIAD OF SANDY BAR

Before nine o'clock it was pretty well known all along the river that the two parties of the "Amity Claim" had quarreled and separated at daybreak. At that time the attention of their nearest neighbor had been attracted by the sounds of altercations and two consecutive pistol-shots. Running out, he had seen dimly in the gray mist that rose from the river the tall form of Scott, one of the partners, descending the hill toward the cañon; a moment later, York, the other partner, had appeared from the cabin, and walked in an opposite direction toward the river, passing within a few feet of the curious watcher. Later it was discovered that a serious Chinaman, cutting wood before the cabin, had witnessed part of the quarrel. But John was stolid, indifferent, and reticent. "Me choppee wood, me no fightee," was his serene response to all anxious queries. "But what did they *say*, John?" John did not *sabe*. Colonel Starbottle deftly ran over the various popular epithets which a generous public sentiment might accept as reasonable provocation for an assault. But John did not recognize them. "And this yer 's the cattle," said the Colonel, with some severity, "that some thinks oughter be allowed to testify agin a White Man! Git — you heathen!"

Still the quarrel remained inexplicable. That two men,

whose amiability and grave tact had earned for them the title of "The Peacemakers," in a community not greatly given to the passive virtues, — that these men, singularly devoted to each other, should suddenly and violently quarrel, might well excite the curiosity of the camp. A few of the more inquisitive visited the late scene of conflict, now deserted by its former occupants. There was no trace of disorder or confusion in the neat cabin. The rude table was arranged as if for breakfast; the pan of yellow biscuit still sat upon that hearth whose dead embers might have typified the evil passions that had raged there but an hour before. But Colonel Starbottle's eye, albeit somewhat bloodshot and rheumy, was more intent on practical details. On examination, a bullet-hole was found in the doorpost, and another nearly opposite in the casing of the window. The Colonel called attention to the fact that the one "agreed with" the bore of Scott's revolver, and the other with that of York's derringer. "They must hev stood about yer," said the Colonel, taking position; "not more'n three feet apart, and — missed!" There was a fine touch of pathos in the falling inflection of the Colonel's voice, which was not without effect. A delicate perception of wasted opportunity thrilled his auditors.

But the Bar was destined to experience a greater disappointment. The two antagonists had not met since the quarrel, and it was vaguely rumored that, on the occasion of a second meeting, each had determined to kill the other "on sight." There was, consequently, some excitement — and, it is to be feared, no little gratification — when, at ten o'clock, York stepped from the Magnolia Saloon into the one long straggling street of the camp, at the same moment that Scott left the blacksmith's shop at the forks of the road. It was evident, at a glance, that a meeting could only be avoided by the actual retreat of one or the other.

In an instant the doors and windows of the adjacent

saloons were filled with faces. Heads unaccountably appeared above the river banks and from behind boulders. An empty wagon at the cross-road was suddenly crowded with people, who seemed to have sprung from the earth. There was much running and confusion on the hillside. On the mountain-road, Mr. Jack Hamlin had reined up his horse and was standing upright on the seat of his buggy. And the two objects of this absorbing attention approached each other.

"York 's got the sun," "Scott 'll line him on that tree," "He 's waiting to draw his fire," came from the cart; and then it was silent. But above this human breathlessness the river rushed and sang, and the wind rustled the tree-tops with an indifference that seemed obtrusive. Colonel Starbottle felt it, and in a moment of sublime preoccupation, without looking around, waved his cane behind him warningly to all Nature, and said, "Shu!"

The men were now within a few feet of each other. A hen ran across the road before one of them. A feathery seed vessel, wafted from a wayside tree, fell at the feet of the other. And, unheeding this irony of Nature, the two opponents came nearer, erect and rigid, looked in each other's eyes, and — passed!

Colonel Starbottle had to be lifted from the cart. "This yer camp is played out," he said gloomily, as he affected to be supported into the Magnolia. With what further expression he might have indicated his feelings it was impossible to say, for at that moment Scott joined the group. "Did you speak to me?" he asked of the Colonel, dropping his hand, as if with accidental familiarity, on that gentleman's shoulder. The Colonel, recognizing some occult quality in the touch, and some unknown quantity in the glance of his questioner, contented himself by replying, "No, sir," with dignity. A few rods away, York's conduct was as characteristic and peculiar. "You had a mighty fine chance:

why did n't you plump him ?" said Jack Hamlin, as York drew near the buggy. "Because I hate him," was the reply, heard only by Jack. Contrary to popular belief, this reply was not hissed between the lips of the speaker, but was said in an ordinary tone. But Jack Hamlin, who was an observer of mankind, noticed that the speaker's hands were cold and his lips dry, as he helped him into the buggy, and accepted the seeming paradox with a smile.

When Sandy Bar became convinced that the quarrel between York and Scott could not be settled after the usual local methods, it gave no further concern thereto. But presently it was rumored that the "Amity Claim" was in litigation, and that its possession would be expensively disputed by each of the partners. As it was well known that the claim in question was "worked out" and worthless, and that the partners whom it had already enriched had talked of abandoning it but a day or two before the quarrel, this proceeding could only be accounted for as gratuitous spite. Later, two San Francisco lawyers made their appearance in this guileless Arcadia, and were eventually taken into the saloons, and — what was pretty much the same thing — the confidences of the inhabitants. The results of this unhallowed intimacy were many subpœnas; and, indeed, when the "Amity Claim" came to trial, all of Sandy Bar that was not in compulsory attendance at the county seat came there from curiosity. The gulches and ditches for miles around were deserted. I do not propose to describe that already famous trial. Enough that, in the language of the plaintiff's counsel, "it was one of no ordinary significance, involving the inherent rights of that untiring industry which had developed the Pactolian resources of this golden land;" and, in the homelier phrase of Colonel Starbottle, "a fuss that gentlemen might hev settled in ten minutes over a social glass, ef they meant business; or in ten seconds with a revolver, ef they meant fun." Scott got a verdict, from which York instantly appealed. It was said that he had sworn to spend his last dollar in the struggle.

In this way Sandy Bar began to accept the enmity of the former partners as a lifelong feud, and the fact that they had ever been friends was forgotten. The few who expected to learn from the trial the origin of the quarrel were disappointed. Among the various conjectures, that which ascribed some occult feminine influence as the cause was naturally popular in a camp given to dubious compliment of the sex. "My word for it, gentlemen," said Colonel Starbottle, who had been known in Sacramento as a Gentleman of the Old School, "there 's some lovely creature at the bottom of this." The gallant Colonel then proceeded to illustrate his theory by divers sprightly stories, such as Gentlemen of the Old School are in the habit of repeating, but which, from deference to the prejudices of gentlemen of a more recent school, I refrain from transcribing here. But it would appear that even the Colonel's theory was fallacious. The only woman who personally might have exercised any influence over the partners was the pretty daughter of "old man Folinsbee," of Poverty Flat, at whose hospitable house — which exhibited some comforts and refinements rare in that crude civilization — both York and Scott were frequent visitors. Yet into this charming retreat York strode one evening a month after the quarrel, and, beholding Scott sitting there, turned to the fair hostess with the abrupt query, "Do you love this man?" The young woman thus addressed returned that answer — at once spirited and evasive — which would occur to most of my fair readers in such an emergency. Without another word, York left the house. "Miss Jo" heaved the least possible sigh as the door closed on York's curls and square shoulders, and then, like a good girl, turned to her insulted guest. "But would you believe it, dear?" she afterwards related to an intimate friend, "the other creature, after glowering at me for a moment, got upon its hind legs, took its hat, and left too; and that 's the last I 've seen of either."

The same hard disregard of all other interests or feelings in the gratification of their blind rancor characterized all their actions. When York purchased the land below Scott's new claim, and obliged the latter, at a great expense, to make a long détour to carry a "tail-race" around it, Scott retaliated by building a dam that overflowed York's claim on the river. It was Scott who, in conjunction with Colonel Starbottle, first organized that active opposition to the Chinamen which resulted in the driving off of York's Mongolian laborers; it was York who built the wagon-road and established the express which rendered Scott's mules and pack-trains obsolete; it was Scott who called into life the Vigilance Committee which expatriated York's friend, Jack Hamlin; it was York who created the "Sandy Bar Herald," which characterized the act as "a lawless outrage" and Scott as a "Border Ruffian;" it was Scott, at the head of twenty masked men, who, one moonlight night, threw the offending "forms" into the yellow river, and scattered the types in the dusty road. These proceedings were received in the distant and more civilized outlying towns as vague indications of progress and vitality. I have before me a copy of the "Poverty Flat Pioneer" for the week ending August 12, 1856, in which the editor, under the head of "County Improvements," says: "The new Presbyterian Church on C Street, at Sandy Bar, is completed. It stands upon the lot formerly occupied by the Magnolia Saloon, which was so mysteriously burnt last month. The temple, which now rises like a Phœnix from the ashes of the Magnolia, is virtually the free gift of H. J. York, Esq., of Sandy Bar, who purchased the lot and donated the lumber. Other buildings are going up in the vicinity, but the most noticeable is the 'Sunny South Saloon,' erected by Captain

Mat. Scott, nearly opposite the church. Captain Scott has spared no expense in the furnishing of this saloon, which promises to be one of the most agreeable places of resort in old Tuolumne. He has recently imported two new first-class billiard-tables with cork cushions. Our old friend, 'Mountain Jimmy,' will dispense liquors at the bar. We refer our readers to the advertisement in another column. Visitors to Sandy Bar cannot do better than give 'Jimmy' a call." Among the local items occurred the following: "H. J. York, Esq., of Sandy Bar, has offered a reward of $100 for the detection of the parties who hauled away the steps of the new Presbyterian Church, C Street, Sandy Bar, during divine service on Sabbath evening last. Captain Scott adds another hundred for the capture of the miscreants who broke the magnificent plate-glass windows of the new saloon on the following evening. There is some talk of reorganizing the old Vigilance Committee at Sandy Bar."

When, for many months of cloudless weather, the hard, unwinking sun of Sandy Bar had regularly gone down on the unpacified wrath of these men, there was some talk of mediation. In particular, the pastor of the church to which I have just referred — a sincere, fearless, but perhaps not fully enlightened man — seized gladly upon the occasion of York's liberality to attempt to reunite the former partners. He preached an earnest sermon on the abstract sinfulness of discord and rancor. But the excellent sermons of the Rev. Mr. Daws were directed to an ideal congregation that did not exist at Sandy Bar, — a congregation of beings of unmixed vices and virtues, of single impulses, and perfectly logical motives, of preternatural simplicity, of childlike faith, and grown-up responsibilities. As unfortunately the people who actually attended Mr. Daws's church were mainly very human, somewhat artful, more self-excusing than self-accusing, rather good-natured, and decidedly weak, they quietly shed that portion of the sermon which referred to themselves, and accepting York and Scott — who were both in defiant attendance — as curious examples of those ideal beings above referred to, felt a certain satisfaction — which, I fear, was not altogether Christian-like — in their "raking-down." If Mr. Daws expected York and Scott to shake hands after the sermon, he was disappointed. But he did not relax his purpose. With that quiet fearlessness and determination which had won for him the respect of men who were too apt to regard piety as synonymous with effeminacy, he attacked Scott in his own house. What he said has not been recorded, but it is to be feared that it was part of his sermon. When he had concluded, Scott looked at him, not unkindly, over the glasses of his bar, and said, less irreverently than the words might convey, "Young man, I rather like your style; but when you know York and me as well as you do God Almighty, it'll be time to talk."

And so the feud progressed; and so, as in more illustrious examples, the private and personal enmity of two representative men led gradually to the evolution of some crude, half-expressed principle or belief. It was not long before it was made evident that those beliefs were identical with certain broad principles laid down by the founders of the American Constitution, as expounded by the statesmanlike A., or were the fatal quicksands on which the ship of state might be wrecked, warningly pointed out by the eloquent B. The practical result of all which was the nomination of York and Scott to represent the opposite factions of Sandy Bar in legislative councils.

For some weeks past the voters of Sandy Bar and the adjacent camps had been called upon, in large type, to "RALLY!" In vain the great pines at the cross-roads — whose trunks were compelled to bear this and other legends

— moaned and protested from their windy watch-towers. But one day, with fife and drum and flaming transparency, a procession filed into the triangular grove at the head of the gulch. The meeting was called to order by Colonel Starbottle, who, having once enjoyed legislative functions, and being vaguely known as "war-horse," was considered to be a valuable partisan of York. He concluded an appeal for his friend with an enunciation of principles, interspersed with one or two anecdotes so gratuitously coarse that the very pines might have been moved to pelt him with their cast-off cones as he stood there. But he created a laugh, on which his candidate rode into popular notice; and when York rose to speak, he was greeted with cheers. But, to the general astonishment, the new speaker at once launched into bitter denunciation of his rival. He not only dwelt upon Scott's deeds and example as known to Sandy Bar, but spoke of facts connected with his previous career hitherto unknown to his auditors. To great precision of epithet and directness of statement, the speaker added the fascination of revelation and exposure. The crowd cheered, yelled, and were delighted; but when this astounding philippic was concluded, there was a unanimous call for "Scott!" Colonel Starbottle would have resisted this manifest impropriety, but in vain. Partly from a crude sense of justice, partly from a meaner craving for excitement, the assemblage was inflexible; and Scott was dragged, pushed, and pulled upon the platform. As his frowsy head and unkempt beard appeared above the railing, it was evident that he was drunk. But it was also evident, before he opened his lips, that the orator of Sandy Bar — the one man who could touch their vagabond sympathies (perhaps because he was not above appealing to them) — stood before them. A consciousness of this power lent a certain dignity to his figure, and I am not sure but that his very physical condition impressed them as a kind of regal unbending and large condescension. Howbeit, when this unexpected Hector arose from this ditch, York's myrmidons trembled. "There 's naught, gentlemen," said Scott, leaning forward on the railing, — "there 's naught as that man hez said as is n't true. I *was* run outer Cairo; I *did* belong to the Regulators; I *did* desert from the army; I *did* leave a wife in Kansas. But thar 's one thing he did n't charge me with, and maybe he 's forgotten. For three years, gentlemen, I was that man's pardner!" Whether he intended to say more, I cannot tell; a burst of applause artistically rounded and enforced the climax, and virtually elected the speaker. That fall he went to Sacramento, York went abroad, and for the first time in many years distance and a new atmosphere isolated the old antagonists.

With little of change in the green wood, gray rock, and yellow river, but with much shifting of human landmarks and new faces in its habitations, three years passed over Sandy Bar. The two men, once so identified with its character, seemed to have been quite forgotten. "You will never return to Sandy Bar," said Miss Folinsbee, the "Lily of Poverty Flat," on meeting York in Paris, "for Sandy Bar is no more. They call it Riverside now; and the new town is built higher up on the river bank. By the bye, 'Jo' says that Scott has won his suit about the 'Amity Claim,' and that he lives in the old cabin, and is drunk half his time. Oh, I beg your pardon," added the lively lady, as a flush crossed York's sallow cheek; "but, bless me, I really thought that old grudge was made up. I 'm sure it ought to be."

It was three months after this conversation, and a pleasant summer evening, that the Poverty Flat coach drew up before the veranda of the Union Hotel at Sandy Bar. Among its passengers was one, apparently a stranger, in the local distinction of well-fitting clothes and closely shaven face, who demanded a private room and retired early to rest.

But before sunrise next morning he arose, and, drawing some clothes from his carpet-bag, proceeded to array himself in a pair of white duck trousers, a white duck overshirt, and straw hat. When his toilet was completed, he tied a red bandana handkerchief in a loop and threw it loosely over his shoulders. The transformation was complete. As he crept softly down the stairs and stepped into the road, no one would have detected in him the elegant stranger of the previous night, and but few have recognized the face and figure of Henry York, of Sandy Bar.

In the uncertain light of that early hour, and in the change that had come over the settlement, he had to pause for a moment to recall where he stood. The Sandy Bar of his recollection lay below him, nearer the river; the buildings around him were of later date and newer fashion. As he strode toward the river, he noticed here a schoolhouse and there a church. A little farther on, the "Sunny South" came in view, transformed into a restaurant, its gilding faded and its paint rubbed off. He now knew where he was; and running briskly down a declivity, crossed a ditch, and stood upon the lower boundary of the "Amity Claim."

The gray mist was rising slowly from the river, clinging to the tree-tops and drifting up the mountain-side until it was caught among these rocky altars, and held a sacrifice to the ascending sun. At his feet the earth, cruelly gashed and scarred by his forgotten engines, had, since the old days, put on a show of greenness here and there, and now smiled forgivingly up at him, as if things were not so bad after all. A few birds were bathing in the ditch with a pleasant suggestion of its being a new and special provision of Nature, and a hare ran into an inverted sluice-box as he approached, as if it were put there for that purpose.

He had not yet dared to look in a certain direction. But the sun was now high enough to paint the little eminence on which the cabin stood. In spite of his self-control, his heart beat faster as he raised his eyes toward it. Its window and door were closed, no smoke came from its adobe chimney, but it was else unchanged. When within a few yards of it, he picked up a broken shovel, and shouldering it with a smile, he strode toward the door and knocked. There was no sound from within. The smile died upon his lips as he nervously pushed the door open.

A figure started up angrily and came toward him, — a figure whose bloodshot eyes suddenly fixed into a vacant stare, whose arms were at first outstretched and then thrown up in warning gesticulation, — a figure that suddenly gasped, choked, and then fell forward in a fit.

But before he touched the ground, York had him out into the open air and sunshine. In the struggle, both fell and rolled over on the ground. But the next moment York was sitting up, holding the convulsed frame of his former partner on his knee, and wiping the foam from his inarticulate lips. Gradually the tremor became less frequent and then ceased, and the strong man lay unconscious in his arms.

For some moments York held him quietly thus, looking in his face. Afar, the stroke of a woodman's axe — a mere phantom of sound — was all that broke the stillness. High up the mountain, a wheeling hawk hung breathlessly above them. And then came voices, and two men joined them.

"A fight?" No, a fit; and would they help him bring the sick man to the hotel?

And there for a week the stricken partner lay, unconscious of aught but the visions wrought by disease and fear. On the eighth day at sunrise he rallied, and opening his eyes, looked upon York and pressed his hand; and then he spoke: —

"And it's you. I thought it was only whiskey."

York replied by only taking both of his hands, boyishly

working them backward and forward, as his elbow rested on the bed, with a pleasant smile.

"And you 've been abroad. How did you like Paris?"

"So, so! How did *you* like Sacramento?"

"Bully!"

And that was all they could think to say. Presently Scott opened his eyes again.

"I 'm mighty weak."

"You 'll get better soon."

"Not much."

A long silence followed, in which they could hear the sounds of wood-chopping, and that Sandy Bar was already astir for the coming day. Then Scott slowly and with difficulty turned his face to York and said,—

"I might hev killed you once."

"I wish you had."

They pressed each other's hands again, but Scott's grasp was evidently failing. He seemed to summon his energies for a special effort.

"Old man!"

"Old chap."

"Closer!"

York bent his head toward the slowly fading face.

"Do ye mind that morning?"

"Yes."

A gleam of fun slid into the corner of Scott's blue eye as he whispered,—

"Old man, thar *was* too much saleratus in that bread!"

It is said that these were his last words. For when the sun, which had so often gone down upon the idle wrath of these foolish men, looked again upon them reunited, it saw the hand of Scott fall cold and irresponsive from the yearning clasp of his former partner, and it knew that the feud of Sandy Bar was at an end.

# HOW SANTA CLAUS CAME TO SIMPSON'S BAR

It had been raining in the valley of the Sacramento. The North Fork had overflowed its banks, and Rattlesnake Creek was impassable. The few boulders that had marked the summer ford at Simpson's Crossing were obliterated by a vast sheet of water stretching to the foothills. The up-stage was stopped at Granger's; the last mail had been abandoned in the *tules*, the rider swimming for his life. "An area," remarked the "Sierra Avalanche," with pensive local pride, "as large as the State of Massachusetts is now under water."

Nor was the weather any better in the foothills. The mud lay deep on the mountain road; wagons that neither physical force nor moral objurgation could move from the evil ways into which they had fallen encumbered the track, and the way to Simpson's Bar was indicated by broken-down teams and hard swearing. And further on, cut off and inaccessible, rained upon and bedraggled, smitten by high winds and threatened by high water, Simpson's Bar, on the eve of Christmas Day, 1862, clung like a swallow's nest to the rocky entablature and splintered capitals of Table Mountain, and shook in the blast.

As night shut down on the settlement, a few lights gleamed through the mist from the windows of cabins on either side of the highway, now crossed and gullied by lawless streams and swept by marauding winds. Happily most of the population were gathered at Thompson's store, clustered around a redhot stove, at which they silently spat in some accepted sense of social communion that perhaps rendered conversation unnecessary. Indeed, most methods of diversion had long since been exhausted on Simpson's Bar; high water had suspended the regular occupations on gulch and on river, and a consequent lack of money and whiskey had taken the zest from most illegitimate recreation. Even Mr. Hamlin was fain to leave the Bar with fifty dollars in his pocket — the only amount actually realized of the large sums won by him in the successful exercise of his arduous profession. "Ef I was asked," he remarked somewhat later, — "ef I was asked to pint out a purty little village where a retired sport as did n't care for money could exercise hisself, frequent and lively, I 'd say Simpson's Bar; but for a young man with a large family depending on his exertions, it don't pay." As Mr. Hamlin's family consisted mainly of female adults, this remark is quoted rather to show the breadth of his humor than the exact extent of his responsibilities.

Howbeit, the unconscious objects of this satire sat that evening in the listless apathy begotten of idleness and lack of excitement. Even the sudden splashing of hoofs before the door did not arouse them. Dick Bullen alone paused in the act of scraping out his pipe, and lifted his head, but no other one of the group indicated any interest in, or recognition of, the man who entered.

It was a figure familiar enough to the company, and known in Simpson's Bar as "The Old Man." A man of perhaps fifty years; grizzled and scant of hair, but still fresh and youthful of complexion. A face full of ready but not very powerful sympathy, with a chameleon-like aptitude for taking on the shade and color of contiguous moods and feelings. He had evidently just left some hilarious companions, and did not at first notice the gravity of the group, but clapped the shoulder of the nearest man jocularly, and threw himself into a vacant chair.

"Jest heard the best thing out, boys! Ye know Smiley, over yar — Jim Smiley — funniest man in the Bar? Well, Jim was jest telling the richest yarn about" —

"Smiley 's a —— fool," interrupted a gloomy voice.

"A particular —— skunk," added another in sepulchral accents.

A silence followed these positive statements. The Old Man glanced quickly around the group. Then his face slowly changed. "That 's so," he said reflectively, after a pause, "certainly a sort of a skunk and suthin' of a fool. In course." He was silent for a moment, as in painful contemplation of the unsavoriness and folly of the unpopular Smiley. "Dismal weather, ain't it?" he added, now fully embarked on the current of prevailing sentiment. "Mighty rough papers on the boys, and no show for money this season. And to-morrow 's Christmas."

There was a movement among the men at this announcement, but whether of satisfaction or disgust was not plain. "Yes," continued the Old Man in the lugubrious tone he had, within the last few moments, unconsciously adopted, — "yes, Christmas, and to-night 's Christmas Eve. Ye see, boys, I kinder thought — that is, I sorter had an idee, jest passin' like, you know — that maybe ye 'd all like to come over to my house to-night and have a sort of tear round. But I suppose, now, you would n't? Don't feel like it, maybe?" he added with anxious sympathy, peering into the faces of his companions.

"Well, I don't know," responded Tom Flynn with some cheerfulness. "P'r'aps we may. But how about your wife, Old Man? What does *she* say to it?"

The Old Man hesitated. His conjugal experience had not been a happy one, and the fact was known to Simpson's Bar. His first wife, a delicate, pretty little woman, had suffered keenly and secretly from the jealous suspicions of her husband, until one day he invited the whole Bar to his house to expose her infidelity. On arriving, the party found the shy, petite creature quietly engaged in her household duties, and retired abashed and discomfited. But the sensitive woman did not easily recover from the shock of this extraordinary outrage. It was with difficulty she regained her equanimity sufficiently to release her lover from the closet in which he was concealed, and escape with him. She left a boy of three years to comfort her bereaved husband. The Old Man's present wife had been his cook. She was large, loyal, and aggressive.

Before he could reply, Joe Dimmick suggested with great directness that it was the "Old Man's house," and that, invoking the Divine Power, if the case were his own, he would invite whom he pleased, even if in so doing he imperiled his salvation. The Powers of Evil, he further remarked, should contend against him vainly. All this delivered with a terseness and vigor lost in this necessary translation.

"In course. Certainly. Thet 's it," said the Old Man with a sympathetic frown. "Thar 's no trouble about thet. It 's my own house, built every stick on it myself. Don't you be afeard o' her, boys. She *may* cut up a trifle rough — ez wimmin do — but she 'll come round." Secretly the Old Man trusted to the exaltation of liquor and the power of courageous example to sustain him in such an emergency.

As yet, Dick Bullen, the oracle and leader of Simpson's Bar, had not spoken. He now took his pipe from his lips. "Old Man, how 's that yer Johnny gettin' on? Seems to me he did n't look so peart last time I seed him on the bluff heavin' rocks at Chinamen. Did n't seem to take much interest in it. Thar was a gang of 'em by yar yesterday — drownded out up the river — and I kinder thought o' Johnny, and how he 'd miss 'em! Maybe now, we 'd be in the way ef he wus sick?"

The father, evidently touched not only by this pathetic picture of Johnny's deprivation, but by the considerate delicacy of the speaker, hastened to assure him that Johnny was better, and that a "little fun might 'liven him up." Whereupon Dick arose, shook himself, and saying, "I'm ready. Lead the way, Old Man: here goes," himself led the way with a leap, a characteristic howl, and darted out into the night. As he passed through the outer room he caught up a blazing brand from the hearth. The action was repeated by the rest of the party, closely following and elbowing each other, and before the astonished proprietor of Thompson's grocery was aware of the intention of his guests, the room was deserted.

The night was pitchy dark. In the first gust of wind their temporary torches were extinguished, and only the red brands dancing and flitting in the gloom like drunken will-o'-the-wisps indicated their whereabouts. Their way led up Pine-Tree Cañon, at the head of which a broad, low, bark-thatched cabin burrowed in the mountain-side. It was the home of the Old Man, and the entrance to the tunnel in which he worked when he worked at all. Here the crowd paused for a moment, out of delicate deference to their host, who came up panting in the rear.

"P'r'aps ye 'd better hold on a second out yer, whilst I go in and see that things is all right," said the Old Man, with an indifference he was far from feeling. The suggestion was graciously accepted, the door opened and closed on the host, and the crowd, leaning their backs against the wall and cowering under the eaves, waited and listened.

For a few moments there was no sound but the dripping of water from the eaves, and the stir and rustle of wrestling boughs above them. Then the men became uneasy, and whispered suggestion and suspicion passed from the one to the other. "Reckon she 's caved in his head the first lick!" "Decoyed him inter the tunnel and barred him up, likely." "Got him down and sittin' on him." "Prob'ly biling suthin' to heave on us: stand clear the door, boys!" For just then the latch clicked, the door slowly opened, and a voice said, "Come in out o' the wet."

The voice was neither that of the Old Man nor of his wife. It was the voice of a small boy, its weak treble broken by that preternatural hoarseness which only vagabondage and the habit of premature self-assertion can give. It was the face of a small boy that looked up at theirs, — a face that might have been pretty, and even refined, but that it was darkened by evil knowledge from within, and dirt and hard experience from without. He had a blanket around his shoulders, and had evidently just risen from his bed. "Come in," he repeated, "and don't make no noise. The Old Man 's in there talking to mar," he continued, pointing to an adjacent room which seemed to be a kitchen, from which the Old Man's voice came in deprecating accents. "Let me be," he added querulously, to Dick Bullen, who had caught him up, blanket and all, and was affecting to toss him into the fire, "let go o' me, you d—d old fool, d' ye hear?"

Thus adjured, Dick Bullen lowered Johnny to the ground with a smothered laugh, while the men, entering quietly, ranged themselves around a long table of rough boards which occupied the centre of the room. Johnny then gravely proceeded to a cupboard and brought out several articles, which he deposited on the table. "Thar 's whiskey. And crackers. And red herons. And cheese." He took a bite of the latter on his way to the table. "And sugar." He scooped up a mouthful *en route* with a small and very dirty hand. "And terbacker. Thar 's dried appils too on the shelf, but I don't admire 'em. Appils is swellin'. Thar," he concluded, "now wade in, and don't be afeard. *I* don't mind the old woman. She don't b'long to *me*. S'long."

He had stepped to the threshold of a small room, scarcely larger than a closet, partitioned off from the main apartment, and holding in its dim recess a small bed. He stood there a moment looking at the company, his bare feet peeping from the blanket, and nodded.

"Hello, Johnny! You ain't goin' to turn in agin, are ye?" said Dick.

"Yes, I are," responded Johnny decidedly.

"Why, wot's up, old fellow?"

"I'm sick."

"How sick?"

"I've got a fevier. And childblains. And roomatiz," returned Johnny, and vanished within. After a moment's pause, he added in the dark, apparently from under the bedclothes, — "And biles!"

There was an embarrassing silence. The men looked at each other and at the fire. Even with the appetizing banquet before them, it seemed as if they might again fall into the despondency of Thompson's grocery, when the voice of the Old Man, incautiously lifted, came deprecatingly from the kitchen.

"Certainly! Thet's so. In course they is. A gang o' lazy, drunken loafers, and that ar Dick Bullen's the orneriest of all. Did n't hev no more *sabe* than to come round yar with sickness in the house and no provision. Thet's what I said: 'Bullen,' sez I, 'it's crazy drunk you are, or a fool,' sez I, 'to think o' such a thing.' 'Staples,' I sez, 'be you a man, Staples, and 'spect to raise h—ll under my roof and invalids lyin' round?' But they would come, — they would. Thet's wot you must 'spect o' such trash as lays round the Bar."

A burst of laughter from the men followed this unfortunate exposure. Whether it was overheard in the kitchen, or whether the Old Man's irate companion had just then exhausted all other modes of expressing her contemptuous indignation, I cannot say, but a back door was suddenly slammed with great violence. A moment later and the Old Man reappeared, haply unconscious of the cause of the late hilarious outburst, and smiled blandly.

"The old woman thought she 'd jest run over to Mrs. MacFadden's for a sociable call," he explained with jaunty indifference, as he took a seat at the board.

Oddly enough it needed this untoward incident to relieve the embarrassment that was beginning to be felt by the party, and their natural audacity returned with their host. I do not propose to record the convivialities of that evening. The inquisitive reader will accept the statement that the conversation was characterized by the same intellectual exaltation, the same cautious reverence, the same fastidious delicacy, the same rhetorical precision, and the same logical and coherent discourse somewhat later in the evening, which distinguish similar gatherings of the masculine sex in more civilized localities and under more favorable auspices. No glasses were broken in the absence of any; no liquor was uselessly spilt on the floor or table in the scarcity of that article.

It was nearly midnight when the festivities were interrupted. "Hush," said Dick Bullen, holding up his hand. It was the querulous voice of Johnny from his adjacent closet: "O dad!"

The Old Man arose hurriedly and disappeared in the closet. Presently he reappeared. "His rheumatiz is coming on agin bad," he explained, "and he wants rubbin'." He lifted the demijohn of whiskey from the table and shook it. It was empty. Dick Bullen put down his tin cup with an embarrassed laugh. So did the others. The Old Man examined their contents and said hopefully, "I reckon that 's enough; he don't need much. You hold on all o' you for a spell, and I 'll be back;" and vanished in the closet with an old flannel shirt and the whiskey. The door closed but imperfectly, and the following dialogue was distinctly audible:

"Now, sonny, whar does she ache worst?"

"Sometimes over yar and sometimes under yer; but it 's most powerful from yer to yer. Rub yer, dad."

A silence seemed to indicate a brisk rubbing. Then Johnny:

"Hevin' a good time out yer, dad?"

"Yes, sonny."

"To-morrer 's Chrismiss, — ain't it?"

"Yes, sonny. How does she feel now?"

"Better. Rub a little furder down. Wot 's Chrismiss, anyway? Wot 's it all about?"

"Oh, it 's a day."

This exhaustive definition was apparently satisfactory, for there was a silent interval of rubbing. Presently Johnny again:

"Mar sez that everywhere else but yer everybody gives things to everybody Chrismiss, and then she jist waded inter you. She sez thar 's a man they call Sandy Claws, not a white man, you know, but a kind o' Chinemin, comes down the chimbley night afore Chrismiss and gives things to chillern, — boys like me. Puts 'em in their butes! Thet 's what she tried to play upon me. Easy now, pop, whar are you rubbin' to, — thet 's a mile from the place. She jest made that up, did n't she, jest to aggrewate me and you? Don't rub thar. . . . Why, dad!"

In the great quiet that seemed to have fallen upon the house the sigh of the near pines and the drip of leaves without was very distinct. Johnny's voice, too, was lowered as he went on, "Don't you take on now, for I 'm gettin' all right fast. Wot 's the boys doin' out thar?"

The Old Man partly opened the door and peered through. His guests were sitting there sociably enough, and there were a few silver coins and a lean buckskin purse on the table. "Bettin' on suthin' — some little game or 'nother. They 're all right," he replied to Johnny, and recommenced his rubbing.

"I 'd like to take a hand and win some money," said Johnny reflectively after a pause.

The Old Man glibly repeated what was evidently a familiar formula, that if Johnny would wait until he struck it rich in the tunnel he 'd have lots of money, etc., etc.

"Yes," said Johnny, "but you don't. And whether you strike it or I win it, it 's about the same. It 's all luck. But it 's mighty cur'o's about Chrismiss — ain't it? Why do they call it Chrismiss?"

Perhaps from some instinctive deference to the overhearing of his guests, or from some vague sense of incongruity, the Old Man's reply was so low as to be inaudible beyond the room.

"Yes," said Johnny, with some slight abatement of interest, "I 've heerd o' *him* before. Thar, that 'll do, dad. I don't ache near so bad as I did. Now wrap me tight in this yer blanket. So. Now," he added in a muffled whisper, "sit down yer by me till I go asleep." To assure himself of obedience, he disengaged one hand from the blanket, and, grasping his father's sleeve, again composed himself to rest.

For some moments the Old Man waited patiently. Then the unwonted stillness of the house excited his curiosity, and without moving from the bed he cautiously opened the door with his disengaged hand, and looked into the main room. To his infinite surprise it was dark and deserted. But even then a smouldering log on the hearth broke, and by the upspringing blaze he saw the figure of Dick Bullen sitting by the dying embers.

"Hello!"

Dick started, rose, and came somewhat unsteadily toward him.

"Whar 's the boys?" said the Old Man.

"Gone up the cañon on a little *pasear*. They 're coming back for me in a minit. I 'm waitin' round for 'em. What are you starin' at, Old Man?" he added, with a forced laugh; "do you think I 'm drunk?"

The Old Man might have been pardoned the supposition, for Dick's eyes were humid and his face flushed. He loitered and lounged back to the chimney, yawned, shook himself, buttoned up his coat and laughed. "Liquor ain't so plenty as that, Old Man. Now don't you git up," he continued, as the Old Man made a movement to release his sleeve from Johnny's hand. "Don't you mind manners. Sit jest whar you be; I 'm goin' in a jiffy. Thar, that 's them now."

There was a low tap at the door. Dick Bullen opened it quickly, nodded "Good-night" to his host, and disappeared. The Old Man would have followed him but for the hand that still unconsciously grasped his sleeve. He could have easily disengaged it: it was small, weak, and emaciated. But perhaps because it *was* small, weak, and emaciated he changed his mind, and, drawing his chair closer to the bed, rested his head upon it. In this defenseless attitude the potency of his earlier potations surprised him. The room flickered and faded before his eyes, reappeared, faded again, went out, and left him — asleep.

Meantime Dick Bullen, closing the door, confronted his companions. "Are you ready?" said Staples. "Ready," said Dick; "what 's the time?" "Past twelve," was the reply; "can you make it? — it 's nigh on fifty miles, the round trip hither and yon." "I reckon," returned Dick shortly. "Whar 's the mare?" "Bill and Jack 's holdin' her at the crossin'." "Let 'em hold on a minit longer," said Dick.

He turned and reëntered the house softly. By the light of the guttering candle and dying fire he saw that the door of the little room was open. He stepped toward it on tiptoe and looked in. The Old Man had fallen back in his chair, snoring, his helpless feet thrust out in a line with his collapsed shoulders, and his hat pulled over his eyes. Beside him, on a narrow wooden bedstead, lay Johnny, muffled tightly in a blanket that hid all save a strip of forehead and a few curls damp with perspiration. Dick Bullen made a step forward, hesitated, and glanced over his shoulder into the deserted room. Everything was quiet. With a sudden resolution he parted his huge mustaches with both hands and stooped over the sleeping boy. But even as he did so a mischievous blast, lying in wait, swooped down the chimney, rekindled the hearth, and lit up the room with a shameless glow from which Dick fled in bashful terror.

His companions were already waiting for him at the crossing. Two of them were struggling in the darkness with some strange misshapen bulk, which as Dick came nearer took the semblance of a great yellow horse.

It was the mare. She was not a pretty picture. From her Roman nose to her rising haunches, from her arched spine hidden by the stiff *machillas* of a Mexican saddle, to her thick, straight bony legs, there was not a line of equine grace. In her half-blind but wholly vicious white eyes, in her protruding under-lip, in her monstrous color, there was nothing but ugliness and vice.

"Now then," said Staples, "stand cl'ar of her heels, boys, and up with you. Don't miss your first holt of her mane, and mind ye get your off stirrup *quick*. Ready!"

There was a leap, a scrambling struggle, a bound, a wild retreat of the crowd, a circle of flying hoofs, two springless leaps that jarred the earth, a rapid play and jingle of spurs, a plunge, and then the voice of Dick somewhere in the darkness. "All right!"

"Don't take the lower road back onless you 're hard

pushed for time! Don't hold her in down hill We'll be at the ford at five. G'lang! Hoopa! Mula! GO!"

A splash, a spark struck from the ledge in the road, a clatter in the rocky cut beyond, and Dick was gone.

. . . . . . . . . . .

Sing, O Muse, the ride of Richard Bullen! Sing, O Muse, of chivalrous men! the sacred quest, the doughty deeds, the battery of low churls, the fearsome ride and gruesome perils of the Flower of Simpson's Bar! Alack! she is dainty, this Muse! She will have none of this bucking brute and swaggering, ragged rider, and I must fain follow him in prose, afoot!

It was one o'clock, and yet he had only gained Rattlesnake Hill. For in that time Jovita had rehearsed to him all her imperfections and practiced all her vices. Thrice had she stumbled. Twice had she thrown up her Roman nose in a straight line with the reins, and, resisting bit and spur, struck out madly across country. Twice had she reared, and, rearing, fallen backward; and twice had the agile Dick, unharmed, regained his seat before she found her vicious legs again. And a mile beyond them, at the foot of a long hill, was Rattlesnake Creek. Dick knew that here was the crucial test of his ability to perform his enterprise, set his teeth grimly, put his knees well into her flanks, and changed his defensive tactics to brisk aggression. Bullied and maddened, Jovita began the descent of the hill. Here the artful Richard pretended to hold her in with ostentatious objurgation and well-feigned cries of alarm. It is unnecessary to add that Jovita instantly ran away. Nor need I state the time made in the descent; it is written in the chronicles of Simpson's Bar. Enough that in another moment, as it seemed to Dick, she was splashing on the overflowed banks of Rattlesnake Creek. As Dick expected, the momentum she had acquired carried her beyond the point of balking, and, holding her well together for a mighty leap, they dashed into the middle of the swiftly flowing current. A few moments of kicking, wading, and swimming, and Dick drew a long breath on the opposite bank.

The road from Rattlesnake Creek to Red Mountain was tolerably level. Either the plunge in Rattlesnake Creek had dampened her baleful fire, or the art which led to it had shown her the superior wickedness of her rider, for Jovita no longer wasted her surplus energy in wanton conceits. Once she bucked, but it was from force of habit; once she shied, but it was from a new, freshly painted meeting-house at the crossing of the county road. Hollows, ditches, gravelly deposits, patches of freshly springing grasses, flew from beneath her rattling hoofs. She began to smell unpleasantly, once or twice she coughed slightly, but there was no abatement of her strength or speed. By two o'clock he had passed Red Mountain and begun the descent to the plain. Ten minutes later the driver of the fast Pioneer coach was overtaken and passed by a "man on a Pinto hoss," — an event sufficiently notable for remark. At half past two Dick rose in his stirrups with a great shout. Stars were glittering through the rifted clouds, and beyond him, out of the plain, rose two spires, a flagstaff, and a straggling line of black objects. Dick jingled his spurs and swung his *riata*, Jovita bounded forward, and in another moment they swept into Tuttleville, and drew up before the wooden piazza of "The Hotel of All Nations."

What transpired that night at Tuttleville is not strictly a part of this record. Briefly I may state, however, that after Jovita had been handed over to a sleepy ostler, whom she at once kicked into unpleasant consciousness, Dick sallied out with the barkeeper for a tour of the sleeping town. Lights still gleamed from a few saloons and gambling-houses; but, avoiding these, they stopped before several closed shops, and by persistent tapping and judicious outcry roused the proprietors from their beds, and made them unbar the doors of their magazines and expose their wares. Sometimes they were met by curses, but oftener by interest and some concern in their needs, and the interview was invariably concluded by a drink. It was three o'clock before this pleasantry was given over, and with a small waterproof bag of India-rubber strapped on his shoulders, Dick returned to the hotel. But here he was waylaid by Beauty, — Beauty opulent in charms, affluent in dress, persuasive in speech, and Spanish in accent! In vain she repeated the invitation in "Excelsior," happily scorned by all Alpine-climbing youth, and rejected by this child of the Sierras, — a rejection softened in this instance by a laugh and his last gold coin. And then he sprang to the saddle and dashed down the lonely street and out into the lonelier plain, where presently the lights, the black line of houses, the spires, and the flagstaff sank into the earth behind him again and were lost in the distance.

The storm had cleared away, the air was brisk and cold, the outlines of adjacent landmarks were distinct, but it was half-past four before Dick reached the meeting-house and the crossing of the county road. To avoid the rising grade he had taken a longer and more circuitous road, in whose viscid mud Jovita sank fetlock deep at every bound. It was a poor preparation for a steady ascent of five miles more; but Jovita, gathering her legs under her, took it with her usual blind, unreasoning fury, and a half-hour later reached the long level that led to Rattlesnake Creek. Another half-hour would bring him to the creek. He threw the reins lightly upon the neck of the mare, chirruped to her, and began to sing.

Suddenly Jovita shied with a bound that would have unseated a less practiced rider. Hanging to her rein was a figure that had leaped from the bank, and at the same time from the road before her arose a shadowy horse and rider.

"Throw up your hands," commanded the second apparition, with an oath.

Dick felt the mare tremble, quiver, and apparently sink under him. He knew what it meant and was prepared.

"Stand aside, Jack Simpson. I know you, you d—d thief! Let me pass, or" —

He did not finish the sentence. Jovita rose straight in the air with a terrific bound, throwing the figure from her bit with a single shake of her vicious head, and charged with deadly malevolence down on the impediment before her. An oath, a pistol-shot, horse and highwayman rolled over in the road, and the next moment Jovita was a hundred yards away. But the good right arm of her rider, shattered by a bullet, dropped helplessly at his side.

Without slacking his speed he shifted the reins to his left hand. But a few moments later he was obliged to halt and tighten the saddle-girths that had slipped in the onset. This in his crippled condition took some time. He had no fear of pursuit, but looking up he saw that the eastern stars were already paling, and that the distant peaks had lost their ghostly whiteness, and now stood out blackly against a lighter sky. Day was upon him. Then completely absorbed in a single idea, he forgot the pain of his wound, and mounting again dashed on toward Rattlesnake Creek. But now Jovita's breath came broken by gasps, Dick reeled in his saddle, and brighter and brighter grew the sky.

Ride, Richard; run, Jovita; linger, O day!

For the last few rods there was a roaring in his ears. Was it exhaustion from loss of blood, or what? He was dazed and giddy as he swept down the hill, and did not recognize his surroundings. Had he taken the wrong road, or was this Rattlesnake Creek?

It was. But the brawling creek he had swam a few hours before had risen, more than doubled its volume, and now rolled a swift and resistless river between him and Rattlesnake Hill. For the first time that night Richard's heart sank within him. The river, the mountain, the quickening east, swam before his eyes. He shut them to recover his self-control. In that brief interval, by some fantastic mental process, the little room at Simpson's Bar and the figures of the sleeping father and son rose upon him. He opened his eyes wildly, cast off his coat, pistol, boots, and saddle, bound his precious pack tightly to his shoulders, grasped the bare flanks of Jovita with his bared knees, and with a shout dashed into the yellow water. A cry rose from the opposite bank as the head of a man and horse struggled for a few moments against the battling current, and then were swept away amidst uprooted trees and whirling driftwood.

. . . . . . . . . . .

The Old Man started and woke. The fire on the hearth was dead, the candle in the outer room flickering in its socket, and somebody was rapping at the door. He opened it, but fell back with a cry before the dripping, half-naked figure that reeled against the doorpost.

"Dick?"

"Hush! Is he awake yet?"

"No; but, Dick" —

"Dry up, you old fool! Get me some whiskey, *quick!*" The Old Man flew and returned with — an empty bottle! Dick would have sworn, but his strength was not equal to the occasion. He staggered, caught at the handle of the door, and motioned to the Old Man.

"Thar's suthin' in my pack yer for Johnny. Take it off. I can't."

The Old Man unstrapped the pack, and laid it before the exhausted man.

"Open it, quick."

He did so with trembling fingers. It contained only a

few poor toys, — cheap and barbaric enough, goodness knows, but bright with paint and tinsel. One of them was broken; another, I fear, was irretrievably ruined by water, and on the third — ah me! there was a cruel spot.

"It don't look like much, that 's a fact," said Dick ruefully. . . . "But it 's the best we could do. . . . Take 'em, Old Man, and put 'em in his stocking, and tell him — tell him, you know — hold me, Old Man" — The Old Man caught at his sinking figure. "Tell him," said Dick, with a weak little laugh, — "tell him Sandy Claus has come."

And even so, bedraggled, ragged, unshaven and unshorn, with one arm hanging helplessly at his side, Santa Claus came to Simpson's Bar and fell fainting on the first threshold. The Christmas dawn came slowly after, touching the remoter peaks with the rosy warmth of ineffable love. And it looked so tenderly on Simpson's Bar that the whole mountain, as if caught in a generous action, blushed to the skies.

# NOTES, COMMENTS, AND QUESTIONS

## JOHN BURNS OF GETTYSBURG

John Burns (1793–1872) had fought in the war of 1812. He was seventy years old when he fought so bravely at Gettysburg.

One of the qualities in human nature that Bret Harte never tires of delineating is that of unaffected virtue. The real hero is he who does his duty naturally; he does not stop to analyze his motives nor to commend — even in thought — his own behavior. Such a hero is the simple-hearted, unimaginative John Burns. It was this trait in human nature of which Wordsworth was thinking when he wrote the *Ode to Duty*.

LINE

2 The assumption of the presence of a listener illustrates the dramatic sense in Bret Harte.

11 **very day.** July 3. The first attack by General Lee was made on July 1. At the end of three days of fighting Lee was forced to retreat with a loss of 30,000 men. The union loss was 23,000.

14 **Meade:** General George Gordon Meade (1815–1872) was in command of the Army of the Potomac at the battle of Gettysburg. Bret Harte makes a rather poor pun on the word *mead*, which he conjoins with field.

15–31 Is the dramatic quality in the character of John Burns increased or diminished by this emphasis upon the old farmer's lack of fancy?

36–54 What details here lend most power to the description of the carnage?

57–69 Of what value is this description of the old man's dress? What does it suggest in reference to his character?

71 **The veterans of the Peninsula** were the soldiers who had been under the command of McClellan while he had been engaged in his campaign in which his objective design was the capture of Richmond.

78 **slangy répertoire:** a storehouse of slang.

89 ff. What was it that finally stopped the scoffs and jeers of the crowd?

LINE

100 Many factions in France opposed Henry IV, known as Henry of Navarre, and leagued their soldiery against him. Led by the Duke of Mayenne these Leaguers attacked the king and his forces at Ivry in March, 1590. Before the battle Henry, with helmet adorned with a large white plume, spoke to his soldiers: "My children, if you lose sight of your colors, rally to my white plume: you will always find it in the path to honor and glory."

Macaulay in his *Battle of Ivry* has told the story most dramatically, putting it into the mouth of a loyal French soldier. The third stanza follows:

The king is come to marshal us, in all his armor dressed,
And he has bound a snow-white plume upon his gallant crest;
He looked upon his people, and a tear was in his eye;
He looked upon the traitors, and his glance was stern and high.
Right graciously he smiled on us, as rolled from wing to wing
Down all our line, in deafening shout, "God save our lord, the King!"
"And if my standard-bearer fall, as fall full well he may, —
For never saw I promise yet of such a bloody fray, —
Press where ye see my white plume shine, amidst the ranks of war,
And be your oriflamme to-day the helmet of Navarre."

108–111 Do you think the poem would be stronger if these last four lines were omitted? Why or why not?

## THE REVEILLE

During the ten years preceding the Civil War, California was a scene of stirring political conflict. Northern and Southern feeling ran high, and it was for a time a serious question whether the State would support the Union. Thomas Starr King was one of the northern leaders who planned a mass meeting in San Francisco just after Lincoln had made his first call for volunteers. He asked Bret Harte to write a poem to be read at this meeting. *The Reveille*, often called *The Drum*, aroused tremendous enthusiasm; the vast audience in one prolonged and universal shout voiced its loyalty to the Union cause, and Bret Harte was its valiant recruiting agent. Neither the urgent demands of the domestic hearth nor the vision of the horrors of the impending conflict, could still the patriotic heart which leaped to respond to the reveille. Few poems of the war period are more spontaneous in their tone.

What is there in the technique of the poem that is admirable?

The patriotic spirit of the Californians of the war period is reflected in two of Bret Harte's stories, — *Mrs. Bunker's Conspiracy* and *Clarence.*

## RELIEVING GUARD

LINE

Thomas Starr King (1824–1864) was a famous Unitarian minister, author, and lecturer. He was born in New York City, but spent most of his life in Boston. Later when he became pastor of a church in San Francisco his most distinguished service was in his successful endeavor to save California to the Union. He was a close friend of Bret Harte, and Bret Harte's second son, Francis King, was given his middle name in recognition of this friendship.

The poem is one of the strongest that Mr. Harte has written. There is deep and intense feeling that is all the more affecting because the concise style holds the emotion in unsevere restraint. The effectiveness is increased by the dramatic conception, the dramatic setting and conversation, and finally by the religious note at the end.

8 Is the pun on the other's name effective? Compare line 14 in *John Burns of Gettysburg.*

## ON A PEN OF THOMAS STARR KING

To the student of American literature King is known by his book, *The White Hills: their Legends, Landscapes, and Poetry,* published in 1859.

## ANNIVERSARY POEM

It is natural that this poem, written a few months after the Civil War, should most strongly reflect the spirit of that unhappy time and contrast the desolation and carnage of the East with the prosperity and peace of the Far West.

1 **native East:** Bret Harte himself was from New York. Many settlers were from New England. Most of them were from the states east of the Mississippi.

4 The **darker tints** were those of blood shed in the Civil War.

14 The **cicala** (chē-kä'lȧ) is the Italian name for the cicada — an insect family represented by the seventeen-year locusts and similar insects.

18 The **long ditch** here referred to holds the water used for irrigating purposes.

19 **sapper:** builder of fortifications.

23, 24 What is the answer to this question?

33, 34 An allusion to the falling walls of Jericho. Cf. Joshua VII, 20.

LINE

45 Cf. Numbers xx, 9–11.

64, 65 An allusion to the rainless season in California.

74–81 Comment on the effectiveness of this simile.

76 **Mariposa:** The county of California in which the Yosemite Falls are situated.

## A SANITARY MESSAGE

There is carried out in *A Sanitary Message* a contrast similar to that in the *Anniversary Poem.* The author is thinking all the time of the sorrows of war that oppress the East. Notice how the military figure is kept up. Name all the varied items and designate their contrasts.

## CHIQUITA

Browning and Bret Harte are both skilled in their handling of the dramatic monologue. The speaker's interposed remarks often suggest but do not exactly specify the actions that go on while the monologue continues. What, for example, is assumed to take place when in line 4 the owner of Chiquita says *Ah, will you, you vixen?*

5 **Morgan:** a breed of horses, famous for their endurance and swiftness.

7 **Tuolumne** (pron. twol′um nē): a county in central California.

9 **savey:** a corruption of the Spanish *saber,* " to know." *Savey* here means knowledge and experience — good sense. What action occasions the remark, — " Quit that foolin' "?

13 **leaders:** the forward pair of horses.

30 The rather grim humor of this line is characteristic of Bret Harte.

## PLAIN LANGUAGE FROM TRUTHFUL JAMES

This poem, popularly known under the title of *The Heathen Chinee,* was first published in the *Overland Monthly* in September, 1870. Its melody (the technical form is borrowed from Swinburne) immediately caught the public ear, and did more than any one thing to make Bret Harte's name familiar to the people.

" Truthful James, himself,[1] who tells the story was a real

[1] Henry C. Merwin: *The Life of Bret Harte,* p. 50.

LINE

character, — nay is, for at the writing of these pages (1911), he still lives in the same little shanty where he was to be found when Bret Harte knew him. At that time, in 1856, or thereabout, Bret Harte was teaching school at Tuttletown, a few miles north of Sonora, and Truthful James, Mr. James W. Gillis, lived over the hill from Tuttletown, at a place called Jackass Flat. Mr. Gillis was well known and highly respected in all that neighborhood, and he figures not only in Bret Harte's poetry, but also in Mark Twain's works, where he is described as 'The Sage of Jackass Hill.' "

There is no deep meaning in the poem; it simply tells a humorous story humorously. Californian duplicity is met by Chinese duplicity, and this last is then dutifully punished by Bill Nye. The swing of the verse is infectious, and there is enough that is clever and peculiar in the phrasing to attract and please. All these facts explain its popularity. It is a pleasure to add that Bret Harte himself always held the poem in slight regard.

## THE SOCIETY UPON THE STANISLAUS

This is one of Bret Harte's earlier poems, written, he tells us, sometime before 1867 and first printed in Ambrose Bierce's *News Letter*.

This poem illustrates in line 28 what is a distinctive phase of Bret Harte's humor, — a tendency not to exaggerate but rather to minimize. Instead of saying that the chunk of red sandstone killed Abner Dean (or perhaps he was not killed, but merely knocked senseless) he cautiously reduces the expression and simply remarks that " the subsequent proceedings interested him no more." However, the minimizing is so strong that it suggests exaggeration.

11 **Brown of Calaveras:** Bret Harte's short story, *Brown of Calaveras*, portrays this character very fully. He is a large-framed man with a character weakened by dissipation.

25 **Abner Dean** appears as a character in two of Bret Harte's stories, *A Monte Flat Pastoral* and *Cressy*.

## A GREYPORT LEGEND

This poem was first published in the *Atlantic Monthly* in 1871. It is one of the few poems in which Bret Harte gives his theme a religious turn. Religion, indeed, seems to have

LINE

had no great dominating influence upon him. In the closing stanza of this poem, however, the cry of the children who are dead seems to beget a faith that draws "the soul to its anchorage."

25 The definite appeal to the sense of sound by the mention of these two items is all the more trenchant because of the brooding silence suggested in line 24.

## SAN FRANCISCO

This poem was Bret Harte's first contribution to the *Overland.* It is a frank admission of the city's faults, its cunning, its greed, its lust, its worship of material grandeur. Yet these do not generate in the writer the feeling of hopelessness for the future. Ultimately Art and Culture will efface all this.

What is the significance of the parenthetical under-title?

5 Comment on the phrase, — *the white seas strike their tents.*

11 **lion's whelp:** The spirit of the city is the spirit of savagery.

18 **skeptic sneer:** her irreligion.

20 **Franciscan Brotherhood:** In Bret Harte's stories there is frequent allusion to Junipéro Serra, the Franciscan friar who was the first Catholic missionary in California.

36 It is apparent that the poet did not expect the regeneration of San Francisco to come during the life of his own contemporaries.

## THE MOUNTAIN HEART'S-EASE

The interesting point in this nature poem is the comparison of the function of the flower with the function of the poet.

## TO A SEA-BIRD

This poem reveals to the imagination a long stretch of beach and sea, the slow sailing or the lazy rocking of the bird, and the lonely poet musing on his limitations. He compares and contrasts his life with that of the sea-bird.

2 In what sense is the bird a vagabond?

3, 4 Is the poet heedless of the surf, the bar, and the shale?

5 Why does the poet ask for this company?

5–10 Is the poet right in considering such a life monotonous?

10–15 What is the limitation of each?

LINE

15–20 Contrast the desire of each.

18 **shingle:** loose gravel and small stones worn smooth by the water.

What do you think of the meter of this poem and its adaptation to the theme?

## WHAT THE CHIMNEY SANG

This poem well illustrates the different feelings which the same phenomenon will arouse in different persons. How do you account for this difference?

5 **forced:** Can you justify the false rhyme?

6 Why did the woman hate the wind?

10–12 Is there any connection between the witch and the fairy?

15 What is your idea of the character and social position of this man?

22, 23 In what way was the poet all three? Of the four, who got most joy from the sound? who got least?

## DICKENS IN CAMP

" When news of the death of Dickens reached Bret Harte he was camping in the Foot-Hills far from San Francisco, but he sent a telegram to hold back for a day the printing of the *Overland*, then ready for the press, and his poem was written that night and forwarded the next morning." — *Merwin.*

There is no question of Bret Harte's admiration for Dickens. Aside from the sincere and tender praise in this poem, there are frequent scenes and passages in his stories which reveal — perhaps unconsciously — the methods and devices of Dickens. And this is a silent but expressive tribute of the younger to the older author. It is pleasant to add to this the regard of Dickens for Harte. Among the last letters that Dickens wrote was one in which he invited Bret Harte to contribute a story to " All the Year Round."

The most marked characteristics of *Dickens in Camp* is the brooding sense of heart-tribute felt in each line. This deep but restrained emotion and the sweet melody of the verse make the poem immortal. The method employed is *tribute by effect.* We are not told directly that Dickens is an interesting story-teller; instead we are made to feel the silent tension of this interest on the faces of the miners grouped about that western camp-fire.

LINE

10 What was the title of this *volume?* Why *hoarded?*

30 Note the significance of the interrogation point.

31 **Kentish:** Dickens's home, during the last ten years of his life, was at Gad's Hill, in Kent.

37–40 Express in your own words the thought of this last stanza.

## THE MISSION BELLS OF MONTEREY

This is the most purely lyrical poem that Bret Harte has written, and is the only one — so far as the present editor is aware — that has been set to music. The composer is Monsieur Charles Gounod.

Monterey is a small village in Monterey County, California. In 1770 the Spaniards established a mission. The picturesqueness of missions appealed strongly to Bret Harte, and he reflects this appeal in this poem, *The Angelus*, and in many of his stories.

Monterey is situated about ninety miles southeast of San Francisco. Here the San Carlos mission was formally established in June, 1770. The bells, brought from Spain, were an important feature. Some were of bronze and others of silver, and there was an effective variety in their tones. The mission during the process of years sunk into decay, but it was restored in 1882.

3 **reddened:** referring to the color of the soil.

5 Explain the line.

6 **Eleison:** In the mass we have the expression, *Christe Eleison!* May the Lord have mercy! Bret Harte uses the word here as an adjective, suggesting that the bells are calling to divine worship.

8–14 Why this discord?

## THE ANGELUS

Bret Harte's interest in the missions is seen in the preceding poem.

The Mission Dolores is often called San Francisco de Asis, after St. Francis of Assisi. The Mission Dolores takes its name from the Dolores — a stream which has since dried up.

18 **Presidio:** a fortified building. Each of these Spanish Missions was protected by military guard. The monks expected to use these soldiers to force conversion of the Indians, if force were

LINE

found necessary. The California Indians were peaceable, however, and were easily converted.

21 **Portolá:** Portolá was the Spanish governor in California at the time of the founding of the first missions. He coöperated with the Franciscan fathers. The Mission Dolores was founded June 17, 1776.

Laura Bride Powers in *The Missions of California* speaks of the quaint adobe chapel of Mission Dolores as " the precious link that joins our civilization of to-day with the romantic mission period."

## THE LUCK OF ROARING CAMP

*The Luck of Roaring Camp* was the first great literary success of Bret Harte's, and from the date of its publication in the *Overland Monthly* in 1868 it has steadily maintained its immediately acquired popularity.

This popularity may be accounted for partly because of its vivid portrayal of California mining life — *local color,* if we wish to employ a very much overworked compound — and partly because of its evidently sincere sentiment. It is probably true that popular taste was caught by the first and has been since held by the second. The story is in Bret Harte's most characteristic vein — it shows elemental virtue existent behind crudeness of manner, dress, and speech. The uncouthness of the mining camp is invested with a certain ideal grace which the presence of a child mysteriously fashions.

PAGE

26 **primal curse:** Cf. Gen. III, 16.

**first transgression:** the eating of the forbidden fruit in the Garden of Eden.

27 **ab initio:** from the beginning.

**putative:** supposed.

28 **until it was lost in the stars above:** phrase effective in enforcing the ascension of the road.

**The pines stopped, etc.:** Find in Bret Harte other examples of the sympathy of nature with the moods of men.

29 **Romulus and Remus:** These legendary founders of Rome were, according to story, suckled by a wolf and thus preserved from death.

**derringer:** a kind of pistol.

**doubloon:** a Spanish coin varying in value from five to fifteen dollars.

PAGE

30 **slung-shot:** a metal ball, with a string attached, used as a weapon.

**rastled:** a corruption of *wrestled.*

32 **"The Coyote":** This animal impressed Bret Harte. Cf. his poem, *Coyote.*

35 **Cockney Simmons:** In *Tennessee's Partner* we get a notion of how names are applied. Simmons was evidently a native of Greenwich, England, and spoke a cockney dialect.

**Mariposas:** Spanish for butterfly. The word is here applied to a kind of flower whose petals have the iris of a butterfly's wing.

36 **albeit there was an infantine gravity, etc.:** This detail is evidently meant to be a slight foreshadowing of Luck's tragic end.

38 Note that Bret Harte does not prolong the conclusion of his story. He closes with the evidence of Kentuck's splendid loyalty and sacrifice, and allows the reader's mind to dwell on that significant detail. The feeling of the camp is evident though unmentioned.

## THE OUTCASTS OF POKER FLAT

Bret Harte as a story-teller sometimes seems as aloof and impersonal as a photographer. In *The Outcasts of Poker Flat* he does not seem to be as much concerned with the desire to portray beauty as he is with the desire to portray truth. If ugliness chances to come within the sweep of his camera and to reveal itself on the sensitized film, Bret Harte does not in the printing blot out the smutches. Uncle Billy is a thief and his thievery is exposed. The Duchess and Mother Shipton show the evil of their past lives. John Oakhurst commits suicide, and this act is frankly revealed. The artist having once chosen a site on which to set up his tripod and camera, lets the mechanism disclose what realities lie within its range. But even so, it is quite evident that the site is chosen with a deliberate plan to hide the most pronounced ugliness and, in the case of the gambler and the women, to picture them at their best. To have pictured them in their entirety would have offended our higher taste. Art is always selective.

It is interesting to note further, that these successive exposures are made not so much to reveal scenes as to reveal character. Nor do we feel that the characters themselves are very different at the end from what they are at the beginning. We simply see them in the fortuitous situation that reveals their charm, their tenderness, their sacrificial intent.

PAGE

*Poker Flat* was in Sierra County, California, and frequently witnessed just such a storm as is here described.

40 **He was too much of a gambler, etc.:** Bret Harte, though never a gambler himself, is fond of portraying the type. There were elements in such gamesters as Jack Hamlin and Mr. Oakhurst that strongly appealed to our author. They were good losers; they were generous; they were free from cant. And these traits certainly are saving graces. Then, too, as long as Bret Harte was portraying the life of the Forty Niners he could not omit the gambler-group.

40 **Parthian volley:** The Parthians, who occupied Parthia, in Asia, were accustomed to shoot their arrows at enemies in retreat. A Parthian shot is, therefore, a parting shot.

44 **Suddenly an idea:** What idea had just come to Uncle Billy?

45 **his usual calm:** Perhaps no trait in Mr. Oakhurst's character is more striking than his calmness. And it is his perfect composure that gives him dominance. Note how it contrasts with the gayety of the Innocent.

46 **cachéd:** hidden.

47 **Covenanter:** The covenanters were a group of Scotchmen strong in their Presbyterian faith who, leagued together stood up stoutly against the oppression of Charles I.

**nigger-luck:** illogically good luck. It was used by the miners to characterize the luck which came to the ignorant and the incapacitated as opposed to the wise and the judicious.

48 **Mr. Pope's ingenious translation of the Iliad:** The term *ingenious* is justified because Pope's translation is very free and inaccurate. The famous remark of Richard Bentley was " a pretty poem, Mr. Pope, but you must not call it Homer."

**argument:** outline of the story.

**son of Peleus:** Achilles. Cf. Classical Dictionary. Note the Innocent's pronunication.

49 Is Mother Shipton's death due to suicide deliberately planned because she wanted release from life; or is it due to her desire to make a sacrifice?

Comment on Bret Harte's skill in portraying character. By what means does he make us feel the supreme domination of Oakhurst over the other members of the company? Note how Piney acts as a character foil to the Duchess and Mother Shipton, and " The Innocent " to Mr. Oakhurst. What is Mother Shipton's favorite way of revealing her animosity to the rulers of Poker Flat? Comment on the part which nature plays in this story. Is the tragic end of the story in anyway forcshadowed?

## TENNESSEE'S PARTNER

PAGE

*Tennessee's Partner* was, like most of Bret Harte's stories, suggested by a real incident, but as the following item from a California newspaper[1] of June, 1903, shows, Mr. Harte has considerably deepened the shadows:

" J. A. Chaffee, famous as the original of *Tennessee's Partner*, has been brought to an Oakland Sanitarium. He has been living since 1849 in a small Tuolumne county mining camp with his partner Chamberlain. In the early days he saved Chamberlain from the vigilance committee by a plea to Judge Lynch when the vigilantes had a rope around the victim's throat. . . . Chamberlain was accused of stealing the miner's gold, but Chaffee cleared him, as every one believed Chaffee. The two men settled down to live where they have remained ever since, washing out enough placer gold to maintain them. . . . Both men are over eighty."

In one of Bret Harte's lectures[2] — the one on the Argonauts — he tells us of the splendid loyalty of the friendships among miners: —

" To be a man's ' partner ' signified something more than a common pecuniary or business interest; it was to be his friend through good or ill report, in adversity, or fortune, to cleave to him and none other — to be ever jealous of him! . . . To insult a man's partner was to insult him; to step between two partners in a quarrel was attended with the same danger and uncertainty that involves the peacemaker in a conjugal dispute. . . . In these unions there were the same odd combinations often seen in the marital relations: a tall and a short man, a delicate sickly youth and a middle-aged man of powerful frame, a grave reticent nature and a spontaneous exuberant one. Yet in spite of these incongruities there was always the same blind unreasoning fidelity to each other."

Bret Harte has revealed this feeling of loyalty in friendship in *Captain Jim's Friend*, *In the Tules*, *Uncle Jim and Uncle Billy*, and in several of his poems, but nowhere are abiding loyalty and elemental stanchness revealed more strongly than in *Tennessee's Partner*. The grimness of the story is relieved by the pathos of masculine devotion — stalwart and undeviating and tender.

[1] See Merwin's *Life of Bret Harte* (p. 165). Houghton Mifflin Company.

[2] Published as an Introduction to *Tales of the Argonauts*. Houghton Mifflin Company.

PAGE

52 **Boston:** Bret Harte uses his characters over and over again. In *The Luck of Roaring Camp* there is a noted wag of this name who prepares the burlesque christening service. There is also a Boston — perhaps the same one — in *The Poet of the Sierra Flat.*

54 **gambler's epigram:** Note in *The Outcasts of Poker Flat,* also, Mr. Oakhurst's expressive gambling metaphors. Bret Harte's friend, Thomas Starr King, the famous San Francisco divine, one Sunday after he had preached a strong controversial sermon overheard an enthusiastic parishioner question a friend, — " Well, what do you think of King now ? " " Think of him," responded his friend, "why, he took every trick."
**chaparral-crested:** Chaparral (Span.) an evergreen oak tree, but used to describe any dense thicket of low bushes.

55 Study the descriptive paragraph at the top of this page and note the skill shown in the selection of items which give significance to the scene.

56 **trousers had been patched:** In Bret Harte's story — *Left out on Lone Star Mountain* — one of the characters is nicknamed " Union Mills," because at one time a patch on his trousers had borne that legend. Cf. the beginning of *Tennessee's Partner* to note how nicknames were often applied.

57 Did the miner offer the money as a bribe, or simply as a recompense for losses?

59 Bret Harte's use of nature is one of the interesting devices employed. Comment on the effect here produced.

60 **sluicing:** a *sluice* or *sluice-box* was a trough used by miners in washing the earth to find gold.
**Jack Folinsbee:** See Bret Harte's *An Heiress of Red Dog* and *The Romance of Madroño Hollow.*
See comment on the second paragraph of this page on page xv of the Introduction.

62 **his face buried in his red bandana handkerchief:** Bret Harte is skilful in the suggestion of pathos; he never allows himself to dwell on pathetic scenes — a glimpse, and the curtain is drawn.

63 Comment on the ending.

## THE ILIAD OF SANDY BAR

This story shows the ultimate loyalty of friendship between partners, — a loyalty triumphing over a long period of separation and hostility. A slight incident — humorous in its triviality — makes the breach, which widens and deepens

PAGE

with the years. The prosperity of York helps finally to soften his belligerent spirit, and he returns to Sandy Bar to seek out his old friend Scott. The story closes with their reconciliation, — grim but complete, — and a smile plays with a deeper emotion as we learn only in the presence of death that the partnership was broken and their lives sundered merely because there was " too much saleratus " in the biscuits which York had baked. The most striking characteristic of the story is the skilful intermingling of sly humor and reserved pathos.

65 **pan of yellow biscuit:** Where is the significance of this detail seen by the reader? Note that Bret Harte by introducing few items into his description of the cabin as it appeared on the morning of the quarrel allows a proper amount of emphasis to fall unobtrusively upon this detail.

**Colonel Starbottle:** One of the most striking and most ubiquitous of Bret Harte's characters. This chivalrous Kentucky colonel plays an important rôle in a score of the author's stories. Bret Harte had written two short paragraphs of *A Friend of Colonel Starbottle's* just before his last illness, but the story, barely begun, remained incomplete.

66 **Jack Hamlin:** He shares with Colonel Starbottle the honor of popularity and frequency of appearance in Bret Harte's stories. His gambling propensities lead him into many scenes and adventures, and through them all he preserves a calmness and a dexterity that win admiration even from his enemies. He is especially popular with women and children.

**said " Shu."** A sly bit of humor that helps to portray the colonel's character.

67 **seeming paradox:** What was the paradox?

**guileless Arcadia:** Explain the sarcasm.

**Pactolian:** pertaining to Pactolus, a river in Lydia whose waters, touched by Midas, made the river sands golden.

68 Emphasis upon the cause of the quarrel helps to increase the humor of the dénouement.

**pretty daughter of "old man Folinsbee":** Old man Folinsbee is a Yankee who moves to California. He appears as a character in *The Romance of Madroño Hollow*. The daughter also figures in the same story. Read the poems *Her Letter, His Answer to her Letter*, and *Her Last Letter*. These all deal with the affairs of Miss Jo Folinsbee and her lover Joe.

72 **philippic:** consult the dictionary for meaning and derivation.

73 **Hector — myrmidons:** Hector, the Trojan, was defeated by Patroclus, the Greek, and his Myrmidons.

PAGE

**Lily of Poverty Flat:** so called in the poem, *Her Letter.*

**'Jo':** the lover of the *Lily of Poverty Flat.*

76 **Sacramento:** where Scott had gone to the legislature after defeating York.

## HOW SANTA CLAUS CAME TO SIMPSON'S BAR

One of the recurring themes in literature is that of sacrifice for the sake of a child's happiness. Whatever is crude, or uncouth or ethically awry in the character of Dick Bullen is immediately pardoned — forgotten almost — because he was willing to undergo hardship and face danger in order that he might give to the little boy at Sandy Bar the joy of those first Christmas toys. The story emphasizes a faith which was inherent in Bret Harte, — the essential virtue and tenderness that a rude environment could not destroy.

78 **Dick Bullen,** "the oracle and leader of Simpson's Bar," is also introduced as a character in *Uncle Jim and Uncle Billy,* where his taunts tend to make Uncle Jim discontented with his life at Cedar Camp.

79 **Tom Flynn:** a Virginia miner who also plays a part in *The Fool of Five Forks.*

82 **a face . . . evil knowledge from within:** When Horace Greeley visited California in 1859 he was particularly impressed with the evils surrounding the children. He saw the need of education and wrote that there ought to be two thousand good common schools in operation but he feared there would not be six hundred. Boys grew up on the streets and were early subjected to the temptation of the evil environment of that rough and irreligious pioneer life.

83 **orneriest:** the superlative of *ornery,* generally explained as a corruption of *ordinary.* The word, however, was always contemptuously applied.

**sabe:** Spanish *saber,* to know; equivalent to *sense.*

84ff. **Oddly enough, etc.:** Mr. Harte's humor is here that of obvious and refined exaggeration.

85 **Why, dad!** Bret Harte's use of pathos is almost always brief and intermittent. He merely suggests the emotion and artistically refrains from dwelling upon it.

**In the quiet, etc.:** note the harmonizing effect of nature's mood.

87 **pasear:** Spanish for *walk* or *promenade.*

87,88 **He turned and reëntered the house:** Study this paragraph to discover the means employed to secure the vivid effect.

PAGE

88 **machillas:** The present editor has been unable to find the exact meaning of this word, as it is explained in none of the reference books to which he has had access. It is probably a hybrid locally used to refer to a portion of the saddle which sits close to the horse's back.

**off stirrup:** right stirrup. The left side of a horse is the *near* side.

89 **Sing, O Muse, etc.:** an imitation of the beginnings of classic epics. Cf. Homer and Virgil.

90 **Pinto hoss:** mottled, piebald. Elsewhere Bret Harte spells it without the capital.

**riata:** lariat.

91 **invitation in "Excelsior."** Cf. Longfellow's *Excelsior:* —

"O stay," the maiden said, " and rest
Thy weary head upon this breast!"
A tear stood in his bright blue eye
And still he answered with a sigh,
Excelsior!

www.ingramcontent.com/pod-product-compliance
Lightning Source LLC
LaVergne TN
LVHW021419110826
845150LV00007B/2000

* 9 7 8 1 4 2 5 5 0 8 7 5 3 *